Towns and Trade
in the
Age of Charlemagne

Duckworth Debates in Archaeology
Series editor: Richard Hodges

Published

Debating the Archaeological Heritage
Robin Skeates

Towns and Trade in the Age of Charlemagne
Richard Hodges

Forthcoming

Loot, Legitimacy and Ownership
Colin Renfrew

Archaeology as Text
John Moreland

Celts, Germans, Scythians and Others
Peter Wells

Towns and Trade
in the
Age of Charlemagne

Richard Hodges

Duckworth

This impression 2003
First published in 2000 by
Gerald Duckworth & Co. Ltd.
61 Frith Street, London W1V 5TA
Tel: 0207 434 4242
Fax: 0207 434 4420
Email: enquiries@duckworth-publishers.co.uk
www.ducknet.co.uk

© 2000 by Richard Hodges

A catalogue record for this book is available
from the British Library

ISBN 0 7156 2965 4

Typeset by
Derek Doyle & Associates, Liverpool
Printed in Great Britain by
CPI Bath

Contents

To Nicole

Tu mea dulcisonis implesti pectora musis
Atque animum moestum carmine mellifluo.

Alcuin, *The Nightingale*

Preface

All those engaged in searching for the truth understand
that the glimpses they have of it are necessarily fleeting.
They glow for an instant and then make way for new and
always more dazzling brightness. Quite different from
that of the artist, the work of the scholar is inevitably
provisional. He knows this and rejoices in it because the
rapid obsoleteness of his books is the very proof of the
progress of his field of knowledge. (Pirenne 1912: 57-8)

There is a simple reason why the archaeology of medieval
European towns has fascinated twentieth-century archaeologists and historians. As Martin Carver vividly puts it, 'the most
visible barometers of investment choice (and therefore of ideological imperative) are the long-lived cities which are still
occupied. The known periods of transition, in the third, fifth,
seventh, ninth and sixteenth centuries, are vital to the story,
even if the result of digging is (sometimes) to find nothing but
black earth' (Carver 1993: 78-9). Having excavated as an
archaeologist in long-lived English towns (Gloucester,
Southampton and Wareham) as well as a deserted ancient city
in Turkey (Knidos), twenty years ago I ventured to contribute
to the debate on the origins of towns and trade in the early
Middle Ages.

Using archaeological models which were stridently positivist
in character, I attempted in *Dark Age Economics* (1982) to rede-
fine a historical controversy which had occupied historians

since the Belgian historian, Henri Pirenne, published his Princeton essays on this theme in 1925. In retrospect my thesis was audacious. Making particular use of a model by the anthropologist Carol A. Smith, I proposed a sequential evolution from pre-market gift-giving economies to dendritic monopolistic markets (emporia) and, following this, to the rise of central-place markets (Smith 1976). The model raised many questions, some of which are still pertinent today. Far from resolving the debate, however, *Dark Age Economics* fuelled discussions which, thanks to a significant number of new archaeological excavations as well as a generation of historians who have begun to appreciate that archaeological evidence provides crucial data about settlement history including consumption, production and distribution patterns, is as lively as it has ever been. Books such as Carver's *Arguments in Stone* (1993), Christie and Loseby's *Towns in Transition* (1995), L. Nilsson and S. Lilja's edited volume *The Emergence of Towns*: *Archaeology and Early Urbanization in Non-Roman, North-West Europe* (1996), Brogiolo and Gelichi's *La Città nell'Alto Medioevo Italiano* (1998) and Brogiolo and Ward-Perkins' *The Idea and Ideology of the Town* (1999) illustrate the enduring intellectual richness of this issue.

This book does not aim to supplant *Dark Age Economics*. Its aim, instead, is to examine four issues which shed light on the continuing debate about the origins of early medieval towns. First, I wish to review the debate itself, reduced as it often has been to binary opposites: archaeologists opposing historians, continuity as opposed to discontinuity, and so on. Second, taking advantage of the fast-growing body of literature on late Roman and early medieval urban archaeology, I want to review the situation in the Mediterranean – a region which, due to the (then) virtual absence of evidence, I omitted from *Dark Age Economics*. Third, I do not intend to review the history of the North Sea emporia in any detail; this I have done in other contexts (Hodges 1982; 1989; Hodges and Whitehouse 1996). Rather, I should like to review the debate about these places as towns, directing the focus away from their role in long-distance trade towards their significance in the creation of regional production and distribution. Fourth, I want to examine how the emporia were abandoned in favour of ranked regional markets.

A version of Chapter 3 appeared in Neil Christie and Simon Loseby (eds), *Towns in Transition*, Aldershot, Scolar Press, 1995. I should like to thank Neil Christie and Simon Loseby for their support and encouragement. I am also grateful for discussions about this theme to the following: Will Bowden, Gian Piero Brogiolo, Martin Carver, Paolo Delogu, Riccardo Francovich, Stéphane Lebecq, John Mitchell, John Moreland, Alessia Rovelli, Lucia Saguì, Adriaan Verhulst, Ian Wood and Chris Wickham. Finally, I wish to thank Deborah Blake at Duckworth for encouraging me to write this book and, as ever, for her constructive criticism at the editorial stage.

Norwich/Tirana 2000 Richard Hodges

1

Binary opposites and paradigms

Rudolf Moosbruger-Leu's objection that 'archaeology has primarily the ethnic aspects of life before its eyes, history has rather the political' is less and less true. More and more, historians look at structures, long-term processes, and other issues previously the domain of ethnography and anthropology. As a result, we are increasingly aware of the limits of our written sources and also that, for much of our work, archaeology is indispensable. The time has come when we can and must work together. (Geary 1991: 45)

Origin myth or geographical premise?

Over the last twenty years medieval archaeology has come out of isolation. It has been widely acknowledged by historians as a valuable source of data, and it has won recognition in most parts of Europe as a critical vehicle for understanding the makings of modern Europe. Moreover the archaeology of post-classical cities has attracted enormous attention. The making of towns, it is now widely accepted, was a critical factor in the making of the Middle Ages. Classical cities, after all, had been instruments of great investment, not just economic centres. Their transformation into new instruments of investment has become one of the main topics in medieval studies. One reason for this has been the growing

11

fascination with the transformation of the Roman world. Another has been the durable fascination with Henri Pirenne's brief overview of the end of classical antiquity and the roots of medieval Europe, *Mohammed and Charlemagne*. The reasons for these fascinations are manifold. Some are explored below. But suffice it at this point to stress that twenty years ago Europe was an uneven political dream, fixed in the minds of politicians, but poorly known to scholars, especially archaeologists who tend to be rooted to archaeological sites in one region, or to cultures that embrace a collection of regions. Today, European integration is becoming increasingly evident in the academic world. Archaeologists in Britain and Italy, Ireland and the Czech Republic, and so forth, are familiar with each other's work, and, above all, aware in the case of urbanism of a shared problem as opposed to something unique to their region.

A number of scholars are concerned that a modern European Union model – a new European origin-myth, centred on the Carolingian empire – is marginalising the sophistication of the Roman achievement, the trauma of its dissolution and the importance of its partial survival. As Brogiolo and Ward-Perkins put it, 'with the declining status of classical education in the modern world, it is not surprising that Rome and its heritage are losing the unifying cultural role that they once played within Europe (both within the former frontiers of the Empire and beyond them)' (Brogiolo and Ward-Perkins 1999: xvi). This book makes no attempt to offer an origin-myth. Indeed, notwithstanding the fact that ninth-century geographers 'regarded the physical Earth not as an independent reality that needed to be studied for its own sake, but as a part of the created world that had to be studied better to understand the Creator' (Lozovsky 1996: 42), the assumption of this book is that the origin of urbanism is a European issue.

1. *Binary opposites and paradigms*

Archaeology and history: binary debates

There is a need for double historicization: first, a historical
contextualization of historical research, i.e. of its concepts
and classificatory schemes .... Second, a historical contextualization of the analysed evidence. (Bourdieu 1996)

According to the famous aphorism of Diogenes Laertius,
'Protagoras asserted that there were two sides to every question
exactly opposite to each other.' It should not surprise us, then,
that historians have argued about two very different trajectories
taken by the flight of time's arrow. The most familiar is
Darwinian gradualism, inescapably associated with the idea of
progress. The other trajectory is known as punctuated evolution.
The latter model, conceived by Niles Eldredge and Stephen Jay
Gould (1972), sets out to explain the abrupt appearance and
subsequent stasis of a species. Punctuated evolution or nongrad-
ualism necessitates a different attitude to the past; it challenges
the idea of linear progress. The human mind, of course, loves
binary opposition. It renders argument clearer. It should not be
surprising that the written sources have a tendency to accentuate
gradual change, whereas the archaeological record, made up of
strata, emphasises intense activity followed by stasis – a punctuated story. Each source poses questions of the other, just as each
has its own ineluctable rhythm. History in its most catholic
sense, as venerated in Clio's great mansion, rests upon exploring
such binary oppositions and constructing hypotheses resting
upon the fruits of debates about them.

Matthew Johnson (1999: 36) in an elegant essay charts these
differences as follows:

Archaeology	History
Artefact	Document
Physical	Symbolic

13

(Objective)	(Subjective)
Vernacular	Elite
Colonised	Coloniser
Long term	Event

Johnson's opposites beg many questions. Reflecting on the growing understanding between archaeologists and historians, between those who examine the elite and the vernacular, the event and the long term, it is important to appreciate how much this binary opposition has, in the past, helped us to shape our modern historical understanding of the formation of European society.

The Dark Age – Renaissance opposition has a long history. As Lawrence Nees has pointed out (1991: 3), a powerful model of European history pays homage to Petrarch's triadic view of history as moving from antiquity, through the Middle Ages, and culminating in *the* Renaissance, with the two good ages on the outside flanking the fideistic obscurantism, unnaturalness, and bad Latin of the negatively defined Middle Age. Yet, Nees points out, the Middle Ages in general and the Carolingian renaissance in particular, unquestionably played a central and indispensable role in continuing and transmitting classical culture. Irked by the continuing, widespread adherence to Petrarch's model, Nees complains of an appalling ignorance about the early Middle Ages, involving a deliberate spurning of the evidence. With some passion he calls for a binary approach that dispels the loaded and pejorative meanings in terms like Dark Age, Medieval and Byzantine and lays emphasis upon our collective debt to Charlemagne. (Will the Charlemagne Prize currently awarded to major European politicians become an important index of achievement or remain merely an obscure marker for a Europe besotted with Leonardo da Vinci and Michelangelo?) This thesis, resonant of *Dark Age Economics*, might be equally applied to Iron Age and early medieval

14

Europe, separated by the aberrant era of the early Roman empire.

Nees, rising to his theme, pointed out in defence of his argument that the adoption of the anno domini system dates from eighth century (Nees 1991: 7). This formative age, unlike *the* Renaissance, signifies the fundamental separation of Christian history from all that went before, as well as the Christian tradition from everything else. This binary theme can be pursued in Charlemagne's own vision of his age. His biographer, Einhard, tells us that the leader's favourite reading was Augustine's *City of God*, in which the late antique author articulated an opposition between the earthly and heavenly city (Dutton 1998: 31). However, whereas the cities of Augustine's lifetime, not least Hippo, his birthplace in North Africa, were palpably cities defined by walls and furnished with streets, public buildings, rich and poor housing, and shops, cities in Charlemagne's time have much less shape in our minds. Quite what binary oppositions came to Charlemagne's mind when he studied Augustine's text – how he envisioned towns in antiquity and his own time – is in effect the quest of this book.

Here it is pertinent to draw attention to Richard Sennett's proposition that the history of the city may be told through people's bodily experience: 'how women and men moved, what they saw and heard, the smells that assailed their noses, where they ate, how they dressed, when they bathed, how they made love' (1994: 15). Sennett also makes use of Augustine's great book. He writes: 'Throughout the *City of God* St Augustine sought to counter these charges that Christianity sickened the Empire. The contrast Augustine drew between the City of Man and the City of God was, indeed, in the words of Peter Brown, "a universal explanation of men's basic motives ... in every age, of a single fundamental tension" (Brown 1967: 321) between the pilgrimage through time and allegiance to place, not a specific repudiation of their own city.' Sennett argues that by the High

Middle Ages urban design was shaped by Christian beliefs about the body. Christ's physical suffering on the cross, for example, offered medieval Paris a way to think about spaces of charity and sanctuary in the city. These spaces, he contends, 'nested uneasily among streets given over to the release of physical aggression in a new market economy' (Sennett 1994: 22). The philosopher John of Salisbury declared in 1159 that 'the state is a body'. He meant that a ruler in society functions just like a human brain, the ruler's counsellors like a heart; merchants are society's stomach, soldiers its hands, peasants and manual workers its feet. 'John connected the shape of the human body and the form of a city: the city's palace or cathedral he thought of as its head, the central market as its stomach, the city's hands and feet as its houses. People should therefore move slowly in a cathedral because the brain is a reflective organ, rapidly in a market because digestion occurs like a quick-burning fire in the stomach' (Sennett 1994: 23). Undoubtedly, the city as a place and institution changed in the age of Charlemagne from the late antique city characterised by Augustine to the precursor of the economic entity described by John of Salisbury.

The enduring debate: re-reading Pirenne

One historian has managed to focus the direction of both archaeologists and historians. As it happens, ever since the publication of Henri Pirenne's short series of lectures entitled *Medieval Cities* (1925), this has been a debate about urban origins.

Pirenne's work has attracted dozens if not hundreds of critiques in the sixty years since his death (Lyon 1974). Along with Marc Bloch's classic study of feudalism, Pirenne's work conjures up a picture of the birth of Europe – an infrastructure that supports the contemporary Franco-German axis that is once again at the heart of European ambitions. Nevertheless, it is only in recent years, looking back as far as his first major paper on medieval urbanism in 1895, that we have begun to command a sufficiently wide-angled view of Pirenne's achievement. Put into context, his thesis throws up many questions that can only be answered as archaeological evidence becomes available to complement the deficiencies of the written sources. There have been many commentaries on Pirenne's thesis, but one merits special attention: Paolo Delogu's (1998a) ambitious re-reading of Pirenne's work offers wide-ranging insights that, far from being irrelevant to our contemporary analysis of the economic and social transformations of the Carolingian age, actually compel us to take a fresh look at the problem.

Delogu argues that Pirenne does not offer a single coherent theory of the relationship between economics and social change. For him the economy provided the essential background within which societies operate, and he could not grasp the ways in which society itself modifies economic structure. In Delogu's view, the reason for this fundamental limitation lies in the gestation of Pirenne's famous thesis. As a young man, in a formative essay in the *Revue Historique* (1895), he identified for the first time the key elements in the origins of medieval urban life as the survival of Roman towns and civic life after the Germanic invasions, and the continuation of strong ties between East and West, broken by the Arab invasions, which precipitated the collapse of the ancient economy and paved the way for the feudalism of the Middle Ages. His 1895 model places emphasis upon the merchant class, the movement of goods and the making of permanent trading-places as the principal elements of change. Mercantilism, in Pirenne's view, was determined not so much by local demand or supply of agricultural goods, as by the necessities of trafficking long-distance goods. Prestige goods exchange – to use the anthropological description – gave birth to the mercantile class which in turn gave birth to the medieval city.

17

Pirenne returned to this subject in 1917 when he was incarcerated in a German internment camp. Here, caught up in the sweep of history, he began his *Histoire de l'Europe*. In this study, undoubtedly influenced by his circumstances, he stressed a progressive degeneration and barbarisation of Roman systems once the classical world was invaded by the Germans. Moreover, throughout this book there is a marked polemical attitude to the Germans themselves, whom he perceived as responsible for the war. It was an attitude he was later to temper in his unfinished, posthumously published book, *Mohammed and Charlemagne* (1939). In 1917, twenty years on from his formative essay on the catalytic importance of the Frankish merchant class, possibly under the influence of the multi-cultural flotsam of his prison camp, Pirenne attributed the revival of trade to impulses coming from the peripheral fringes of the West: Venice and parts of southern Italy as well as the Viking raiding and trading between Byzantium and the shores of the North Sea. These two currents of traffic penetrated into continental western Europe – the heartlands of Francia, Austrasia and Neustria – reaching northern France and Flanders. These sporadic impulses drew new subjects to the trading enterprises and, as a result, created a new social class of professional merchants. The substance of this 1917 model is that the economy was driven by agriculture and organised within a framework set by seigneurial landlordship: the so-called 'agrarian economy'. In sum, with the disappearance of markets in the West following the closing down of the Mediterranean, profit, in Pirenne's opinion, ceased to be the prime mover of economic activity. As a result, agriculture and other forms of production were tailored to local consumption.

Pirenne's 1917 model was a volte-face. Whereas his 1895 model had challenged Karl Buecher's interpretation of closed economy in *Zur Entstehung der Volkswirtschaft* (1893), in 1917 Pirenne, possibly swayed by the exigences of camp life, paid homage to this central idea, rejecting Alfons Dopsch's erudite survey of the problem in *Wirtschaftsentwicklung der Karolingerzeit* (1913) which ascribed primacy to the vitality of commerce. As to the causes of change, Pirenne appeared to give credence to the role of chance in history.

After the First World War Pirenne did not publish his History of Europe. Instead he quarried it for two studies, 'Mahomet et Charlemagne' and 'Un contraste économique: merovingiens et carolingiens', published in the *Revue Belge de Philologie et d'Histoire* in 1922 and 1923 respectively. In these celebrated essays he contended that the heartland of European civilisation was relocated in the regions between the Seine and Rhine, while Mediterranean regions were a periphery. The 1922-23 model, of course, owed everything to the previous century: the roots of nineteenth-century geopolitical supremacy of the Franco-German nucleus of Europe was to be found in an age inaugurated by the Carolingians. The argument was doubtless prompted by Dopsch's rebuttal of Pirenne's 1895 analysis. Dopsch maintained that no caesura or interruption occurred between the Roman and Carolingian ages. Hence Charlemagne's achievement did not initiate the new circumstances as Pirenne believed. In his 1922-23 essays, Pirenne argued that Carolingian economics consisted of a mosaic of restricted economies and of a largely inconsequential flow of precious commodities. Successive recessions caused by the progress of the Islamic conquest of the Mediterranean regions in the seventh and eighth centuries accounted for the rupture between antiquity and the Carolingian age.

A decade later Pirenne returned to the matter for the final time, drafting his celebrated monograph *Mohammed and Charlemagne* (1939). His objective was largely to re-state the thesis presented in his seminal essay of 1922, with one significant difference. Underlying the book was a description of how a new Europe was forged, not merely in economic terms, but also in political, social and cultural affairs. The context, after all, was the fomenting age of the League of Nations as well as the rise of Communism, Fascism and Nazism. In Pirenne's reductive vision the crisis of the ancient order caused new political forces to supplant their moribund predecessors. Adaptation to the changed circumstances was fundamental, as best illustrated by the Austrasians, the Germanic community least affected by the crises afflicting late antique and even Merovingian institutions. In *Mohammed and Charlemagne* he introduces a significant new element in the ascendency of the Carolingians – the history of the papacy. Abandoning their former ties with the Byzantine East in the eighth century, the popes redirected their interests northwards, seeking alliances with the Carolingian kings. This volte-face had far-reaching implications. Notably, an unitary cultural ethos drawn from the long traditions of the Roman church now underpinned the new (Germanic) aspirations of this Europe. Islam, in this version, separated the Christian church of Rome from Constantinople, propelling it closer to Charlemagne's ambitions. As Delogu concludes, 'Pirenne explicitly asserted his conviction that movement in history is caused by the human will, being the product of the conscious intention and action of individuals or social groups .... *Mahomet et Charlemagne* is a history of the birth of Europe as a political and ideological entity, although in the field of economics Dark Age Europe remained primordial' (1998a: 38). Can we really doubt that *Mohammed and Charlemagne*, a most contentious and provocative reading of the transformation of the Roman world, was fundamentally a lifetime's reaction to the rise of Europe's bitterly divided nations in the 1930s following the intense Bismarckian nationalism of the later nineteenth century and the incomprehensible tragedy of the First World War?

Delogu's re-reading is an outstanding if dispassionate essay

on an eminent forebear. Like so many (almost all?) late twentieth-century historians, he is puzzled by all the fuss about
Pirenne and the enduring fascination for his flawed ideas.
Historians invariably distrust 'the vision thing' (to use modern
jargon). Moreover, it is clear that Pirenne's 1895, 1917, 1922-23
and 1939 models are variations on a theme of Arab causality
which are plainly wrong. This said, Delogu reads Pirenne from
an Italian standpoint, detached from the thrust of Pirenne's
Franco-German axis, and, as is commonly the case today, barely
touched by its contemporary significance as once again a new
Europe takes shape. Nevertheless, Delogu recognises that the
majestic sweep of Pirenne's history retains a timelessness that
finds a resonance in modern scholarship, quite unlike Gibbon's
Decline and Fall. It belongs to a time when Europe was
painfully aware of its Continental proportions, yet still vague
about regionalism, not so far removed from the sub-Roman and
Carolingian periods. Not least, it describes the setting in which
Rome tellingly looked north in 800 for the first time in its
history, as the architectural historian Richard Krautheimer
noted (1980), and took its cue from courts situated in the Rhine-
Seine triangle.

Each of Pirenne's models contains elements that can be
tested, now that there is archaeological evidence to complement
the scanty written sources. For example, his first model,
published in 1895, sets up two key issues:

(i) Roman towns and civic life were broken by the Arab not the
    Germanic invasions
(ii) the merchant class and the movement of goods led to the
    establishment of permanent trading-places and ultimately
    towns

As we have already noted, by 1917 Pirenne ascribed the revival
of trade to two currents of traffic:

(i) from Venice and southern Italy
(ii) from the shores of the North Sea

These impulses led to

(iii) a new social class of professional merchants
(iv) trade was not the prime mover of economic activity; the economy was driven by agriculture and organised within a framework of seigneurial landlordship.

By 1922-23 he had elaborated his ideas to place stress upon:

(i) the Seine-Rhine region as the heartland of European civilisation by AD 800
(ii) much of the rest of Latin Christendom consisted of a mosaic of restricted economies loosely connected by a largely inconsequential flow of precious commodities

Finally, in *Mohammed and Charlemagne* he introduces:

(i) the papacy in a critical alliance with the Carolingian kings as a fundamental feature in the Carolingian renaissance.

Reduced to these bald hypotheses, it is evident why Pirenne's thesis has remained so contentious. The written sources, for the most part, are silent on these matters. Only occasional references shed light on merchants (1895), the movement of goods (1895), long-distance trade emanating from the peripheries of Christendom – Venice, southern Italy, the shores of the North Sea (1917) and the mosaic of closed regional economies. Inevitably, generations of twentieth-century historians from Dopsch to the present have been tempted to interpret the problem as created by the sources. As many written documents were destroyed by the Arab and Viking assaults on southern and northern Europe in the later ninth century, it is tempting, since many medieval towns occupy the same sites as their Roman forebears, to postulate a continuity of civic life. No one, of course, doubts the ascendency of the agrarian economy by the ninth century. But the supply of and demand for agricultural products had to be focussed somewhere; old Roman civic centres provided the context.

Twenty years ago the archaeological sources were sufficiently ample in the Mediterranean and north-west Europe to bring a new measure of analysis to the problems posed by Pirenne. Excavations in old Roman cities and ports around the Mediterranean charted a history at variance with the chronology dependent upon the rise of Islam described by Pirenne. Meanwhile, the importance of long-distance trade around the shores of the North Sea was especially clear from large-scale excavations at places such as Dorestad (Netherlands), Haithabu (Germany), Hamwic (United Kingdom), and Ribe (Denmark). It was also evident that the Carolingian renaissance, drawing upon an alliance with the papacy, had far-reaching effects encompassing not just major architectural projects but also significant developments in minor arts and crafts. Yet the archaeological sources were far from comprehensive. Excavations of post-classical (eighth- and ninth-century) sites around the Mediterranean were relatively rare before the 1980s. Indeed, excavations of Middle Byzantine and Arabic sites are few even today. Nevertheless, excavations in southern Italy, Rome, Lombardy and Venice shed fresh light on Pirenne's sequence of models.

Moreover, whereas there were a dozen or so excavations of Carolingian-period rural sites in, say, 1980, today the number exceeds a hundred. Added to this, many regional studies, paralleling those made by historians, shed new light on the mosaic of territories. The results are truly illuminating. There is no doubt that the Dark Ages, the caesura with Roman civilisation, was more complex and regionally varied than anyone had imagined.

An older generation of historians, wary of the peculiarly British, even Victorian use of 'Dark Ages', is understandably challenged by the new data. This generation was raised on the primacy of the written sources and, above all, the sheer wealth of variety of these sources in the Seine-Rhine region as well as in places like Rome. A Dark Age inevitably flies in the face of such civilised riches. It suggests discontinuity, primitiveness and the loss of civilised behaviour. Many historians, nurtured in sheltered university libraries and muniment rooms, can readily empathise with the authors of their written sources, but find it impossible to comprehend how these sources could have been produced in anything other than civilised circumstances. Pirenne's stature rests on the fact that he could imagine a discontinuity of European civilisation as early as 1895, which he then personally experienced during the First World War. A century or so later, with the availability of measured archaeo-logical data from a great variety of sites – not only elite sites where the written sources were composed, but minor sites where the peasantry, largely denied history, lived – it is clear that the configurations of Europe in the Carolingian age were complex.

Pessimists and optimists

The question of continuity or discontinuity, according to Bryan Ward-Perkins in an entertaining essay on early medieval towns in northern Italy (1997), can be summed up as a debate between pessimists and optimists. The pessimists (apparently I fall into this group: Ward-Perkins 1997: fig. 4) favour 'cata-strophe', or to be more precise, some discontinuity between Roman and medieval towns in Italy, whereas the optimists favour unbroken continuity between the two periods. (The debate in Italian archaeology in the 1990s broadly mirrored

that in Britain in the 1980s; see Astill 1985.) Ward-Perkins
writes as follows:

> In the hands of different writers, even a very similar
> image can be used to very different effect. Wickham, for
> instance, in 1981 summed up his impression of early
> medieval housing, based at this date almost exclusively on
> charter evidence, in the following words: 'Private housing
> seems often to have been in wood, and set back from the
> road, with a courtyard in front and a garden behind,
> looking perhaps more like a run-down garden suburb than
> like Pompeii.' The image is quietly unpretentious, and
> derives from the English idyll of a Ford Fiesta in the front
> drive and neighbours, not too close, over the garden fence.
> Apart from the adjective 'run-down', the wording could
> almost come out of an estate agent's window in the Home
> Counties. In 1994 Carandini, presumably after a visit to
> the USA, used a closely comparable image to argue the
> opposite point: 'A certain level of intense activity and
> maintenance is essential to the city, and where it is
> lacking, as today in some North American centres, the city
> dies or is transformed into one of those suburban settle-
> ments of houses with gardens, which resemble compacted
> bits of countryside rather than true and proper cities'. In
> one memorable sentence, Carandini, who presumably
> prefers the roar of traffic to that of the lawnmower,
> dismisses the leafy suburbs of America and the garden
> cities of England, and, with them, casts early medieval
> Lucca out beyond the pale of true urbanism. (Ward-
> Perkins 1997: 167)

Ward-Perkins is graphic about the divide which separates
scholars: it boils down to what might euphemistically be
described as a misunderstanding between two entrenched acad-

emic animals – archaeologists and historians. Historians, he argues, approach the problem through contemporary texts, and find in these continuous references to *civitates*, and to a *civitas*-based ecclesiastical and secular administration. 'If what is excavated does not look very "city-like", then it is our expectations of a town that must change. For who are we to gainsay the opinion of contemporaries?' (Ward-Perkins 1997: 168). Archaeologists, on the other hand, he asserts, are naturally more trusting of things as evidence. He cites our understanding of sterile black earth, the soil accumulation that suggests abandonment often found separating Roman and medieval occupation levels, and post-holes, the features usually interpreted as remains of post-built timber buildings. Why archaeologists should be 'naturally more trusting of things' is a little baffling, though it fulfils Johnson's expectations, tabulated above, that archaeologists are interested in the physical while historians favour the symbolic. But surely Ward-Perkins ventures a little too far when he writes that archaeologists 'with considerable justification, ... are suspicious of words and texts, as ideological constructs designed to deceive as much as to inform' (1997: 168). Apparently, archaeologists find the hard evidence of the soil more reliable than written sources and, dare one say, these curious creatures obtain 'some pleasure ... in almost literally rubbing the noses of historians in the dirt and squalor of the post-Roman town'. Historians, he acknowledges, 'with their texts are not always kind to archaeologists with their supposedly humbler pots; there is therefore some pleasure to be derived from exposing the textual *civitates* of the historians as miserable collections of run-down huts' (ibid.: 169). This well-informed caricature brings to mind a recent critique of contemporary history by Eley and Nield: 'A theoretical *hauteur* instructs a redoubt of methodological conservatism, and the latter shouts defiantly back. Between the two lies a silence, a barrier that in these tones cannot be crossed' (Eley and Nield 1993: 221). Yet drawing up the disciplinary draw-bridge, as Richard J. Evans puts it in his recent textbook on history, has never been a good thing for historians (1997: 8).

Just as archaeologists must look beyond the limits of their trenches, so historians must beware of being too bookish. After half a century of large-scale archaeological interventions, the material sources are now beginning to offer substantive infor-mation for historians raised on textual histories. Moreover, with the considerable publication of reports and essays on medieval archaeology during the last twenty years, there is much for the historian to study in the comfort of the library. Patrick Geary, an American teaching medieval history in the USA, seems near the mark when he argues, in the case of medieval religious history, 'To borrow an expression anthropologists have used to contrast contemporary non-western religions with postreform and counterreform Christianity, medieval religion was not believed but danced. To understand the "steps" of this dance, the archaeologist must distinguish the essential structures unifying this material and establish, as it were, a model of a system of functional and representational interdependences among his sources. The textual historian must do the same. The two models must be juxtaposed and combined and only then compared with the articulated reflections of elite cultural tradi-tions' (Geary 1991: 44). This seems an appropriate direction, looking beyond polarised approaches.

Paradigms and methodological considerations

The much loved topic of 'continuity' can now come off the agenda altogether (Carver 1993: 61).

The archaeology of early medieval towns is not the caricature presented by Bryan Ward-Perkins. Before the Second World War, there were virtually no stratigraphic excavations of

Roman and medieval towns. The forum of Rome, for example, was cleared of all the levels post-dating the first century AD in several campaigns of excavations. Only random notes and photographs bear witness to the later Roman and early medieval levels which were rudely removed. Even the excavations in the 1920s of the early medieval emporium at Dorestad by Holwerda were undertaken by workmen clearing arbitrary levels and recording the data in what the anthropologist Clifford Geertz calls 'thick description' (Geertz 1973). The large-scale excavations undertaken for the SS at the Danish emporium of Haithabu, near Schleswig, on the eve of the Second World War mark the first use of stratigraphic excavations in urban archaeology. As it happened G.C. Dunning was carrying out small-scale stratigraphic investigations in the city of London in the late 1930s, but, unlike Haithabu, these results were not put to some wider historical purpose. After the Second World War the technique of stratigraphic excavation was introduced in North Africa by the British School at Rome with the investigation of cities such as Leptis Magna and Sabratha. At the same time a new generation of archaeologists was using these techniques in bomb-damaged cities such as Southampton (to excavate the Middle Saxon town of Hamwic) and Xanten in Germany. But the scale of these excavations was extremely limited. The prevailing instrument of analysis was the trench, a few metres long by a few metres wide. The practice of open-area excavation, used on rural sites in Denmark and the Netherlands before the Second World War, and steadily developed on rural sites in Britain in the 1950s, was not adopted in the complicated, multi-period circumstances of a city until the early 1960s when Martin Biddle experimented with stripping a sector of Winchester, the capital of Wessex. Biddle's bold use of open-area excavation effectively changed the analytical filter employed by archaeologists. Hitherto, restricted to small cuttings through complex palimpsests of layers, archaeologists placed emphasis upon chronology and debated the issue of continuity of occupation. Open-area excavation made it possible to reconstruct the changing topography of a town through time. Dorestad, the early medieval emporium first investigated by Holwerda in the early 1920s, was the most ambitious venture using this new method. Armed with a special machine for clearing large areas, Wim van Es, Director of the Dutch State Archaeological Service, uncovered several hectares in a celebrated salvage project between 1967 and 1977 specifically to identify the topographic axes of the emporium. Van Es's method was a controversial advance, laying emphasis upon the macro-detail of the town as opposed to the micro-data of the tenemental plot (Hodges 1999). The outcomes of these great projects are still not fully published, such was the immense amount of information unearthed. Winchester studies, like the Dorestad publications, are in progress. Both excavations, however, gave rise to countless other projects all over Europe during the 1970s and early 1980s which were amply published during the later 1980s and especially the early 1990s, when funds for expensive large excavations were more difficult to obtain.

The town of Brescia, one of the places that figures prominently in Ward-Perkins' analysis cited above, is just such a site. Thanks to the energetic efforts of Gian-Pietro Brogiolo, a large sector of the Roman and medieval town was not only systematically excavated, but has also been the subject of numerous analytical studies. An insula of the wealthy Roman city, occupied by a town house furnished with elegant mosaics, witnessed a long sequence of later occupation, including late Roman post-built structures cutting the mosaic pavements, sixth- to seventh-century Lombard-period sunken huts, and, ultimately, a monastery that from the mid-eighth century, when it obtained royal patronage, prospered and evolved on this site. Similarly, the current excavations in the heart of Rome are revealing much the same story, while indicating what was unceremoniously removed during the clearance of the Forum in the early decades of the twentieth century. Already it is evident how the great early imperial public monuments were transformed in late antiquity, and fell into disrepair during the later sixth century. Thereafter, amongst the ruins were sustained islands – small palaces, modestly repaired monasteries and churches, and small aggregations, it is surmised, of simple town housing. Half a kilometre away, in the area of the Campus Martius, complex open-area excavations in the early 1980s by Daniele Manacorda and Lucia Saguì (1995) revealed how a great classical monument became a waste-land intermittently used by glass-makers in the fifth century, then for several centuries a place for rubbish dumping by an adjacent monastery.

Archaeology, with the investigation of these places, has offered historians real measurements. The changing scale of urban and economic life, revealed in these carefully unearthed examples, is indisputable.

This applies also to those parts of the Carolingian world where the written sources are almost non-existent, such as Ireland and Scandinavia (Hines 1994; Nilsson and Lilja 1996; Clark 1998). Clark (1998: 339), for example, rightly points out that the much-studied emporium at Kaupang in southern Norway was, in fact, little more than a *vicus* (see Hodges 1982: 81; Blindheim, Heyerdahl-Larsen and Tollnes 1981; Blindheim and Heyerdahl-Larsen 1995). In other words, he has in mind the kind of traders' quarters situated outside the gates of great monasteries such as St Denys or San Vincenzo al Volturno (Hodges 1997: 116). To describe such places as proto-urban or proto-towns, however, is a classic historians' fudge (Hodges 1982). These are centres with specific settlement characteristics (including measured evidence of the scale of production and distribution) which permit us to situate them in regional exchange systems either as nodes in dendritic systems with

1. Binary opposites and paradigms

monopolistic (gateway) centres, solar central-place systems or competitive market systems (Hodges 1982).

In a nutshell, therefore, the scientific methods of urban archaeology in the twentieth century have comprised three stages:

(i)   Clearance excavations (by workmen)
(ii) Stratigraphic trenching (by archaeologists and students)
(iii) Open-area excavation (by professional archaeologists)

The results of the third stage, open-area excavation, are little short of revolutionary. This book is essentially devoted to describing the main lines of this revolution. But before developing this theme, a short parenthesis is needed. Each of these stages, as we shall see, gives rise to a new paradigm, calling to mind Thomas Kuhn's *The Structure of Scientific Revolutions* (1962). In place of the existing view (in the 1950s) of science as continuous progress, Kuhn argued that most scientists worked, often unconsciously, within a paradigm or set of assumptions which determined their experiments and ensured that their observations matched their theories. Thus paradigms could not be falsified, and problems, where the data did not fit the paradigm, were usually ignored. Only when the problems accumulated to a point at which they generated unease in the scientific community did the search for a new paradigm commence. The great disadvantage of a new paradigm was that it might fail to account for some phenomenon that the old one succeeded in explaining. And different paradigms belonged to different cognitive circumstances, which were not necessarily comparable with one another. Science, in Kuhn's analysis, was not necessarily progressive, but maintained by intellectual consensus. Historians as a rule do not subscribe to Kuhn's notion of scientific paradigms; they tend to work with less rigid and constricting historical interpretations (Evans 1997: 42-3).

Yet Kuhn's proposition is a satisfactory tool for evading the thorny question whether history is a science. It is clear that history, and indeed the history of archaeological ideas about post-classical urbanism, based upon the discovery and existence of archaeological evidence obtained by one of at least three methods, has not followed a linear progression but a series of steps akin to a succession of paradigms. These are as follows:

(i) [Clearance excavation] The debate about urban continuity-discontinuity
(ii) [Stratigraphic trenching] The debate about long-distance as opposed to regional exchange
(iii) [Open-area excavation] The debate about agency: what purposes did urban centres serve?

The aim of this book, drawing upon the increasing use of contemporary archaeology, is to develop a re-reading of Pirenne's thesis about the origins and nature of ninth-century towns in western Europe. Essentially, three questions will be investigated:

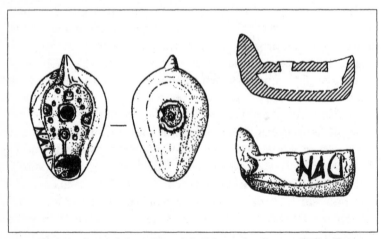

Fig. 1.   An eighth-century lamp from the Crypta Balbi, Rome
(after Ceci 1992).

1. Binary opposites and paradigms

(i) Was there a revival of trade in the Mediterranean in the eighth and ninth centuries which gave impulse to the economic and social ambitions of the Carolingian age?

(ii) What agencies led to the birth of medieval towns?

(iii) What form did towns take in the ninth century (during the so-called Carolingian renaissance) as regional production and distribution increased in western Europe?

2

Charlemagne's elephant

Discontinuity

> Our theme must be discontinuity; the only issue is which.
> People have argued for millennia over exactly what
> changed as the Roman world turned into the Middle Ages
> in the different parts of the empire; but what no one has
> ever been able to argue away is that there *was* a break of
> some kind, perhaps of many kinds, at the end of Antiquity.
> (Wickham 1994: 99)

Post-classical Europe took shape as the Arab empire first
consolidated control from the Euphrates to Spain, and then,
halted at the Battle of Poitiers by Charles Martel, fostered
internal developments which, under a succession of Abbasid
caliphs, put it at the centre of connections reaching from
Canton in China to Aachen in Frankia. The history of investment in urbanism in the Mediterranean, as Henri Pirenne
recognised, cannot be detached from the wider historical and
geographical context of this region. Pirenne and his critics have
suffered from having a eurocentric viewpoint; they have
suffered too from the impoverishment of sources – written
histories which carefully edit out references to non-Christians;
urban archaeology which has evolved at different rates with
little or no sound stratigraphic evidence from classical or
Islamic towns until the last decade or so. Yet the history of the
Carolingians, and quite possibly the history of urbanism, is to

35

some extent bound up with the history of the Abbasids, papal Italy and Byzantium. One familiar illustration confirms this point.

Harking back to the age of Augustus, the story of Charlemagne's elephant is an issue of entanglement reaching across ideological divisions. The debate about Charlemagne and town-making in western Europe has been tied to an eurocentric view of the later eighth and ninth centuries. In 792, with the opening up of Canton's harbour to Arab merchantmen, the West gained first-hand experience of T'ang dynasty China. Arabic glass was carefully exported eastwards in return for silks and other exotica. Cities many times larger than Samarra in the Abbasid caliphate or Constantinople flourished in China. What has this to do with western Europe, and Charlemagne in particular? The answer is that Latin Christendom was not an island. The Carolingian king was clearly intrigued by the East. Indeed, around the year 800 the Abbasid caliph Harun al'Rashid sent an embassy to Charlemagne. Led by the governor of Egypt, Ibrahim Ibn al-Aghlab, the Arabs brought a special gift from the master of the Moslem world to the supreme ruler of Latin Christendom: an elephant called Abu l'-Abbas. The elephant had been originally owned by an Indian rajah before being acquired by Harun's predecessor, caliph Al-Mahdi.

The Abbasid mission was a response to an embassy despatched by Charlemagne to the caliph's court in 797 – the first of three embassies sent to the caliphate (the others set out in 802 and 807 respectively). The Arabs crossed the Mediterranean and disembarked at Pisa. From there, in part following the old Via Cassia, their journey led over the the Alps to Charlemagne's court in the Rhineland. Once in Germany, Charlemagne presumably built a house for Abu l'-Abbas, where the creature lived for the best part of a decade. We know only one further detail of its colourful life. The *Frankish Annals* record that when King Godfred of the Danes seized traders from *Reric* – possibly old Lubeck – and installed them at *Sliastorp* (possibly the archaeological site known as either Haithabu or Hedeby), Charlemagne took the elephant with him on his march to quell the trouble. The two great casualties of the campaign were Godfred, who was assassinated during a revolt in the Danish camp, and Abu l'-Abbas. The elephant died at Lippeham on Luneburg Heath.

The story of the elephant draws the thinnest of historical threads together, forging connections between the Arabs, Latin Christendom and the Vikings: between Moslems, Christians and Nordic pagans, setting in motion a cycle of entangled relations. But we should be cautious of taking the story at face value. In 1813, when Sir Stafford Raffles sent a Javanese elephant to the Japanese emperor, a fine woodblock print records the impact it made, even though it proved impossible to disembark the creature. Inevitably Harun's gift raises many questions: what kind of boat was used to carry the beast to Pisa, for it could not have been accommodated on any of the known late Roman or high medieval wrecks so far discovered in Mediterranean waters? Are we to assume that the deep-draughted cargo vessel could be docked against a quay at Pisa (unlike Raffles' ship when it reached Nagasaki)? How did the envoys progress to Germany? Did Charlemagne build elephant houses at his palaces of Ingelheim, Aachen and Nijmegen? How did the elephant, a tangible commodity from another ideology, influence his attitudes to that ideology and, consequently, contribute to the re-examination of his own ideology? Was it old Roman imperial vanity that persuaded him to take the creature on the Danish campaign?

Such questions are unlikely to be answered. The Arab boat was probably a one-off. Was the quay in Pisa a relic of Roman times or a timber-framed version like those now well-known from North Sea ports? The details of the journey, doubtless the subject of much contemporary discussion in Italian and transalpine courts, are lost forever. The remains of the elephant house(s) are unlikely to be discovered in the built-up centres which now close in around the palatial courts once inhabited by Charlemagne and his entourage. Charlemagne's opinions of Islam is unknown. Indeed, almost nothing is known of Carolingian attitudes to Islam, except that churches in Rome and monasteries such as Monte Cassino and San Vincenzo al Volturno actively acquired Arabic exotica whenever possible. As for Charlemagne's vanity, we can only speculate on the old warrior's tetchy reactions as this arthritic master of much of Europe received word of the Dane's impudent actions.

As a historical episode, the voyage begs many questions. Since 1895 when Pirenne first challenged the notion of trade across the Mediterranean basin after the Islamic conquests of the seventh century, this illustration of an embassy with a vessel large enough to carry an elephant has seemed intriguing. Plainly, it flies in the face of a powerful historical paradigm. Familiar as we have been with Arabic coins (dirhems) as well as other oriental objects in ninth-century Viking contexts as a result of trade connections between the Abbasids, Rus and the many argonauts of the Baltic sea, contact between Latin Christendom and the Arabs, following Pirenne's thesis, has nevertheless always been interpreted as minimal (Noonan 1994). Those sailing in Mediterranean waters, so the sources indicate, were mostly pilgrims bound for the Holy Land (McCormick 1998). But could it be that the written sources for ideological reasons – the proscribed heresy of intercourse between Christians and Arabs – have concealed the true nature of contact across the Mediterranean? Further, given that the Arabic objects from the Baltic Sea region occur mostly in pagan graves and ports, might the archaeological evidence also be deceiving us? After all, Christian graves in Latin Christendom were seldom graced with accoutrements in this period, and the great port cities of the Mediterranean, including Pisa where the

38

elephant disembarked, have received only minimal archaeological attention.

The elephant is intriguing for another reason. As a gift it was a classical symbol of regal authority, conspicuously lending an exoticism to its imperial owner. Harun al'Rashid's gift to Charlemagne, however, is by no means an unique act of largesse. Silvio Bedini's study of Pope Leo X's elephant provides a useful indication of an elephant's status in pre-modern times (1998). King Manuel I of Portugal despatched an elephant to the pontiff in 1514. The creature was named Hanno and achieved great popularity in Rome. There are accounts of Hanno's acrobatic tricks, while the Pope wrote Latin sonnets to him and charged artists with making paintings and sculptures of his pachyderm gift. The Pope was grief-stricken at Hanno's death. Appreciating this, Manuel I, intent on demonstrating his growing claims to the new discoveries in the East, despatched a rhinoceros to Rome. Unfortunately, the boat carrying the beast foundered and the animal drowned. Yet, as if to illustrate the symbolism of the gift, efforts were made to retrieve the corpse of the rhinoceros, which was stuffed and delivered to the Holy City. Like Hanno, Charlemagne's elephant was a symbol of the search for connections, arguably as the European world of gift-giving experienced a renaissance of commodification in tandem with a cultural renaissance (Hodges 1982; Hodges 1997; Hodges and Whitehouse 1996). Like Hanno, Charlemagne's elephant carried echoes of the imperial grandeur associated with the great Roman emperors who deployed such beasts in the vanguards of their conquering armies as well as at displays in Rome itself.

Charlemagne's elephant, taking into account its implicit connections as well as the entangled symbolism of the gift, inevitably brings to mind the central tenets of Pirenne's classic book *Mohammed and Charlemagne* (1939). Pirenne's theme, reviewed above in Chapter 1, is that dramatic changes in the

Mediterranean at the end of the Roman age isolated the Merovingian kings in north-west Europe and led to the gradual rise of the Carolingians, who were economically remote from the Mediterranean. Similarly, the isolation of Italy compelled the Pope to ally himself with the aspiring Carolingian dynasty in the later eighth century. This led to the coronation of Charlemagne as emperor in Rome on Christmas Day, 800. Pirenne felt that these events had profound effects upon the embryonic medieval economy and, significantly, set the scene for the Carolingian cultural renaissance. Accordingly, he concluded: 'It is therefore strictly correct to say that without Mohammed Charlemagne would have been inconceivable. In the seventh century the ancient Roman Empire had actually become an Empire of the East; the Empire of Charles was an Empire of the West .... The Carolingian Empire, or rather, the Empire of Charlemagne, was the scaffolding of the Middle Ages' (Pirenne 1939: 174). Was a policy of urban renewal part of this scaffolding?

The end of antiquity

Pirenne's belief that the Arabs disrupted Mediterranean trade, separating the Roman world from the Carolingian one, has long since been disproved. The transformation of the regions around the Mediterranean for the most part happened before the seventh-century Arab expansion. Indeed, it could be argued – contentious though this might be – that the Arabs were responding to a vacuum created by a steady and inexorable decline of Roman life around the Mediterranean.

The picture of decline grows ever more complex with each new excavation. The predominant picture is of a region which fragmented into a patchwork of areas linked by dwindling political and economic connections. A good place to witness this transformation is Butrint in southern Albania – more or less in

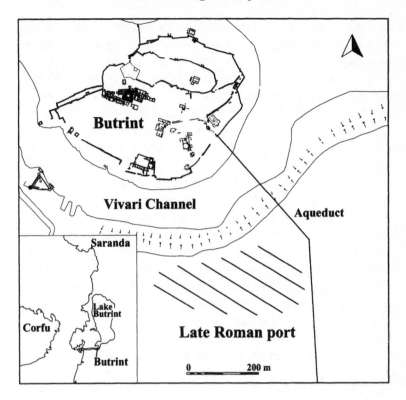

Fig. 2. A plan of Butrint in all periods showing the location of the
Late Roman port.

the middle of the Mediterranean (Hodges et al. 1997). The
Graeco-Roman port situated on the straits of Corfu had prospered since the fourth century BC, enjoying the double benefits
of being on the north-south route up the Adriatic and on the
east-west route between the Balkans and southern Italy.
Towards the end of the fifth century AD, in common with many
Epirote towns, a massive investment programme was launched.
Kilometres of new fortifications were erected, while inside the
town a palace, a new cathedral and a conspicuously grand

41

baptistry were built. Concurrently many areas within the old Roman public buildings were now occupied by earth-bonded dwellings of an immodest architectural quality. Evidently, despite Gothic incursions in the Balkans, the city had the means to support a large population. The Byzantine apogee was short-lived. While the baptistry remains a minor jewel in the many architectural and artistic achievements of the Justinianic age, the neighbouring palace was never completed. Twenty years ago we would have supposed that the Slavs simply overwhelmed the town as they swept down the Balkan littoral in the later sixth century. The archaeological stratigraphy, however, reveals a different story. The palace was left unfinished, but soon occupied by householders living in small earth-bonded structures not uncommon in modern post-communist Albania. Their rubbish middens tell us a little about them. East Mediterranean and Spanish amphorae sherds are mixed with a few fragments of Cypriot red-slipped tableware and Syrian glass. In addition, there are large amounts of locally produced pots besides red-painted vessels possibly made in southern Italy. In amongst this voluminous rubbish is a fragment of a so-called Slavic brooch. The middens span about fifty years, terminating towards *c.* 625, when the archaeological sequence ends, interrupted until the later tenth or eleventh century.

The great curtain walls at Butrint, in common with the refortification of other cities in Epirus such as Byllis, Nicopolis and Phoenicê, reveal the last major public efforts in this region around AD 500. Butrint's apogee was the Justinianic age, but it continued to participate in a vibrant local and seaborne economy for a further century.

Not every town, however, had such a history. Saranda, ancient Onchesmus, 19 kilometres north of Butrint, occupied a mere 4-5 hectares in late antiquity, a quarter of the area occupied by Butrint (Hodges et al. 1997: 214). Nevertheless, it too was fortified in the age of the Emperor Anastasius, towards the end of the fifth century. Extensive layers of burning in the excavations here, however, show that the town was sacked in the 570s, almost certainly by the Slavs. While Butrint was to flourish modestly throughout the Middle Ages up until the Ottoman occupation, Saranda passed into oblivion.

The late antique picture of Butrint and Saranda offers a vignette of life around the Mediterranean, during and after the upheavals caused by massive Byzantine investment in advance of invaders. Klavs Randsborg has illustrated this transformation as the gradual but inexorable shift of power from Rome to Constantinople, creating new peripheries which, as power then dwindled in Constantinople, suffered their own decline (Randsborg 1991). Hence, by AD 600 the economic energy of the coastal littorals of the central and western Mediterranean was largely exhausted, replenished by contact with the east Mediterranean. Soon, though, the winds of change overwhelmed the heartlands of Byzantium, and its cities experienced the same reduction and decline of economic and social activity.

Excavations at Sardis have uncovered a fascinating window on this twilight of the Roman age. In contrast to the fifth- and sixth-century shops in Butrint constructed inside the ruined fabric of the city, at Sardis – as was the case in many western Anatolian towns – new streets of purpose-built shops were being erected (Crawford 1990). Similar streets have now been identified in other great cities of the east Mediterranean – Jerash and Palmyra, to name only two instances. The architectural formula is not so different from the shops at Ostia and Pompeii built more than half a millennium earlier. Sardis's shops have a small portico separating them from the wide, paved street. In *c.* 616 they were destroyed in a devastating fire, possibly the result of a Persian attack. Of all the shops E13 is perhaps the most revealing. Over 350 window panes and 350 goblets were discovered in the excavation of the ruins. On the eve of the conflagration the shop-keeper was evidently furnishing fellow-citizens with panes to repair their dwellings as well as a rich array of 'up-market' tablewares. The excavated evidence indicates the capacity to produce ample capital in nearby workshops as well as the shop-owners' cash-flow capacity to purchase such a volume of merchandise. Shop-life in Sardis in the early seventh century was bouyant at a time when, to take two examples of many, craftsmen were virtually camping in the ruins of the Crypta Balbi (Saguì 1998a) – the exedra of the great theatre of Balbus in the Campus Martius at Rome – or occupying makeshift market stalls in the degenerated ruin of the forum of Cherchel (Potter 1995), once a great Roman port in North Africa. The latter craftsmen, invariably described as 'squatters' by the archaeologists who discovered their remains, were as much part of the declining late Roman world as the shop-keepers of Sardis.

As the decline continued, so shanty-like buildings began to occupy the western Anatolian towns. By about AD 640 window panes were no longer repaired. Sardis, in other words, had become like Butrint, Cherchel and indeed, the down-at-heel conditions in the heart of Rome itself (Potter 1995). In this twilit world the production of many commodities persisted. New research shows that African red slipware dishes were made in Tunisia up to the arrival of the Arabs in the last decade of the seventh century (Saguì 1998b). Although the great ports of this North African coastline had long since fallen into sharp decline, and notwithstanding the concomitant loss of markets in southern France and Italy, some tablewares were made for those 'squatters' who continued to sustain the barest modicum of Roman civic life. It is a history which has many parallels. Local pottery production persisted throughout the coastal regions of the Mediterranean, albeit on a much reduced scale. This much is clear from pottery sequences now known in the Algarve, south-eastern Spain, Rome, Naples, the Apulian

44

littoral, and a few centres in Greece and Cyprus. Cooking-pots and amphorae altered modestly in form, though in many regions hand-made wares were also introduced in this age. The volume of production, understandably, diminished dramatically (Saguì 1998b).

The entangled circumstances of decline are growing ever more familiar (Brogiolo and Gelichi 1998; Brogiolo and Ward-Perkins 1999). Less familiar are beacons of continuity. Urban life continued in the two great capitals of Constantinople and Rome in the eighth century. But where else?

Townlife in the eighth century

John Haldon has cogently summarised the differences between the typical late Roman city and the medieval town: 'public buildings were no longer funded from "public" sources'. The role of the city corporations was taken over by the Church and by monasteries, by private individuals, or by other associations. By the seventh century new urban construction, Haldon contends, was primarily facilitated by the Church (Haldon 1999: 21; 1990: 153-72; 395-9). The so-called senatorial aristocracy of the late Roman world was replaced during the seventh century by a new elite. Haldon pinpoints the 650s and 660s as the decades when a large number of 'new men' – a kind of state meritocracy selected by emperors on the basis of their skills and expertise – came to power. Power, as a result, was increasingly invested in the emperor and the authority of the state. Not surprisingly, in the face of entrenched opposition from the landed aristocracy outside this new circle of power, the court created a new cultural consciousness – 'a world view in which Constantinople and imperial patronage, on the one hand, and provincial roots and identities, not associated with cities and civic pride, on the other, played the key role' (Haldon 1999: 20). So began the age of iconoclasm which effectively isolated

Byzantium as a buffer state between the Arabs and Latin Christendom.

In this era, the historian Wolfram Brandes argues, there was *the* city, Constantinople, and only four or five other settlements which could lay claim to the title (Thessaloniki, Ephesus, Nicaea and Trebizond) (Brandes 1999: 25). Taking account of the limited written sources, Brandes distinguishes the concept of the multi-functional role of a town from the more specific function of a fortress or a village.

The city, Constantinople, undoubtedly outlived the crisis of urbanism in the West. Nevertheless, the city of a million or more inhabitants in the fifth century was probably reduced to a tiny fraction of that figure by 717 when it was vigorously invested by the Arabs (Mango 1985: 54). Stratigraphic excavations at the Great Palace and Saraçhane show beyond doubt the continuity of town life. Harrison's important excavations at the church of St Polyeuktos (Saraçhane) show that everyday commodities, available in the fifth and sixth centuries in some volume, continued to be available in the eighth and ninth centuries (Harrison 1986; Hayes 1991). Coarse pottery altered little in form; fine pottery was scarce, but by the ninth century glazed wares were obtainable (Hayes 1992). Glass lamps and lamp chains altered in form but were available. Craft production and distribution, the notable feature of places such as Butrint and Sardis before AD 600, continued to exist. What remains uncertain is whether the shops of late antiquity continued to function or, whether Constantinople was, like Rome, a city full of secular and ecclesiastical nuclei which, as in the case of the active monastery on the edge of the Campus Martius in Rome, produced commodities for its own use and small amounts for directed exchange.

Thessaloniki, Ephesus, Nicaea and Trebizond may have continued as central-places on a smaller scale. Clive Foss's classic study of Ephesus, however, shows that the eighth- to ninth-century town was reduced to a hilltop site, a shadow of the sprawling late Roman metropolis (Foss 1979; Haldon 1999: 16 n. 43). Survey and excavation suggest that it was divided into three small, distinct and separate zones – a fortress/administrative centre, church and market town. What is now evident is that almost all the other great cities and ports of the region were reduced to fortresses, even more modest in scale than that at Ephesus (Haldon 1999: 16 n. 43). Sardis shrank to a small fortified acropolis like Ephesus with one or more separate occupied areas within the original wall circuit. Miletos was reduced to some twenty-five per cent of its original area and divided into two defended complexes. Perhaps the most illuminating recent archaeological discovery in this regard has been made in the Anatolian fortress cities of Ancyra and Amorion.

In common with most Byzantine cities, Ancyra shrank to a small citadel during the 650s and 660s (Haldon 1990: 112-13; 1999: 14). The fortress occupied an area measuring 350 × 150 metres (Lightfoot 1998). Amorion had a *kastron* occupying some 450 × 300 metres; in 716 it was attacked by an army of many thousands and successfully defended by 800 men. Excavations within the *kastron* by Chris Lightfoot have shown that, while the late antique town was very extensive, with circuit walls and towers as impressive as any in Anatolia, the occupied areas were similar to those of Ancyra. The evidence shows that 'while the very small fortress-citadel continued to be defended and occupied, discrete areas within the late Roman walls also continued to be occupied, often centred around a church' (Haldon 1999: 15). Small, poorly made town houses constructed of rubble, *spolia* and mud have been unearthed (Lightfoot 1998: fig. 8). The associated material culture, in common with Constantinople, shows the continuity of commodity production (coarse pottery, transport amphorae, lamps, lamp chains, etc.).

The discoveries at Amorion, modest though they appear by

classical standards, are of great significance because, apart from small groups of pottery from temporary settlements (as in the case of the eighth- to ninth-century occupation in the orchestra of the ancient theatre at Sparta (Waywell and Wilkes 1995)), all Byzantine settlement in the Balkans and Anatolia was reduced to hilltop nuclei like Amorion (Foss 1977; Spieser 1989; Hodges and Whitehouse 1996). Amorion is an invaluable model, and notwithstanding Brandes' hasty (to use his adjectival criticism of archaeologists) historical reading of the excavation reports ('I would nevertheless be very surprised if Amorion was to be *the* exception in the development of settlements in the seventh and eighth centuries' (Brandes 1999: 40)), it is to be hoped that the excavations of the site are completed in coming years.

Haldon provides a valuable description of the communities who lived in these places (1999: 15-16): 'I would suggest that what we are confronted with here are small but distinct communities whose inhabitants regarded themselves (in one sense, that of domicile, quite legitimately) as "citizens" of the city within whose walls their settlement was located; that the *kastron*, which retained the name of the ancient *polis*, provided a refuge in case of attack (although in many such cases it may not necessarily have been permanently occupied, still less permanently garrisoned); and that therefore many of the *poleis* of the seventh to ninth centuries survived as such because their inhabitants, living effectively in distinct villages within the area delineated by the walls, saw themselves as belonging to the *polis* itself, rather than to a village.'

To date the archaeological evidence indicates that this markedly reduced manner of *kastron* living remained until commerce in the eastern Mediterranean took off in the early eleventh century, largely articulated by Arab traders in Egypt and Palestine. Byzantium appears to have had a highly entrenched, statist economy, unlike Latin Christendom (Haldon 1999: 19).

2. Charlemagne's elephant

This reduction of townlife to citadels did not occur in Palestine. Towns had prospered in the Levant in the seventh century, weathering the transformation from Byzantine to Umayadd rule (Foss 1997; Kennedy 1985a; 1985b; Pentz 1992; Walmsley 1995). But with the transformation, Palestine found a new energy and looked eastwards rather than towards the Mediterranean. The most celebrated symbol of this energy is the remarkable planned town of 'Anjar, situated close to Baalbek in what was Greater Syria and is today the Lebanon. 'Anjar is dated by a series of Syriac graffiti left by Kurdish workers in the quarry from which its best stone came up to AD 714. 'Anjar was almost equidistant from Damascus, then the Umayyad capital, and Berytus (modern Beirut), the nearest suitable port to Damascus. Quite probably Beirut was of great strategic importance to the caliphate in its persistent struggle with Byzantium for mastery of the eastern Mediterranean.

The impressive ruins plainly sustain the tradition of classical construction. They comprise a large rectangular enclosure measuring 370 × 310 metres (an area of 11.4 hectares) with attached hydraulic works pertinent to managing its agricultural resources. The town consists of an attached palace, mosque, residential and presumably administrative quarters and commercial structures (probably shops of the Sardis type) (Hillenbrand 1999). The settlement appears to have been built and abandoned within the space of forty years.

The classical plan of 'Anjar is bisected by a colonnaded *cardo* running north-south and a *decumanus* running east-west. These two axial streets intersect in the centre of the town, a spot marked by a purely classical tetrapylon, the forerunner, Hillenbrand proposes, of the Islamic market crossing (1999: 62). The south-west quadrant contained the principal area of habitation, though traces of town-houses have come to light in the north-west quadrant. Some 114 shops can be seen, concentrated on either side of the city's colonnades. Hillenbrand

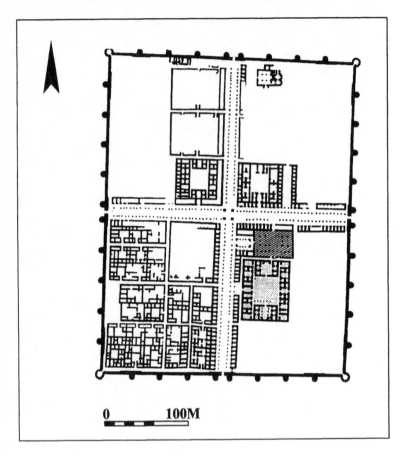

Fig. 3. A plan of 'Anjar *c.* 750 (after Hillenbrand, 1998).

speculates that twice as many shops may have been planned. A mosque and palace dominate the south-east quadrant, while the northern half of 'Anjar contains two well-preserved courtyard buildings. Near the north gate is a large bathing complex, probably for public as opposed to royal use. As yet the extensive excavations made in the town have not been published, so the history of 'Anjar, however brief, is relatively unknown. Hillenbrand ventures an interpretation of the plan as follows:

- The concept of the rectilinear grid underpins the plan
- Provision for concentrated housing is confined to a single quadrant
- Official and religious functions are concentrated to a quadrant
- Planning of the site seems not to have been 'envisioned as an integrated entity, but rather to have proceeded piecemeal in discrete, ... unrelated blocks' (1999: 65)

He believes the rectilinear grid to be modelled upon a Roman *colonia*, an illustration of Umayyad fascination with Rome as a world empire safely in the past. However, a case has been made in the past for its model being an exceptionally large Umayyad palace – a case rejected by Hillenbrand. He favours 'Anjar being the work of an architect, still constrained within the framework of classical architecture, groping his way towards the definitive solution of an Islamic city, Baghdad – a city which was to be completed within fifty years (Hillenbrand 1999: 76).

'Anjar is a failed town. Surrounded by swampland at the time, it is difficult to envisage how its plethora of shops could have prospered. Others in this region that succeeded – Antioch, Damascus, Edessa – illustrate the persistence of townlife, and the shift from classical planning to the distinctive Islamic formula with its central marketplace, the *suq* (Ward-Perkins 1996: 148-52). This Islamic formula was embodied in the design of Baghdad, a city founded in 762. This signal transformation, though, bids us to note one significant point. From colonnaded shops to *suq*, 'Anjar and its peer towns were provisioned by their architects with the intention of functioning as market centres. From the limited archaeological evidence of commodity production in the region after the seventh century, it appears

that, in common for example with Constantinople, craft indus-
tries were not extinguished (Foss 1997). Unlike Byzantium, the
Umayyad dynasty evidently had a vision of economic growth
sustained by managed towns. Can we doubt that pilgrims from
Latin Christendom – who had travelled via the emporium of
Quentovic on the English Channel along Roman roads littered
with ruins, through the desolation of Rome itself, and onwards
– were hugely impressed by the vision?

How much this Umayyad vision affected Spain, a region
closer to Latin Christendom, is not yet clear. A new generation
of Spanish archaeologists has begun to provide a picture of
urban continuity and discontinuity following the Islamic
conquest of the Iberian peninsula after AD 711. Rather as in
Palestine, craft production appears to have persisted, albeit at a
comparatively low level. In southern Spain and southern
Portugal, some towns may have continued as centres in this era,
though many of the great classical centres from the region of
Murcia-Alicante up to Catalonia were evidently deserted (see
Gutiérrez Lloret 1998; Gomez Becerra 1995; Scales 1997).

Italy, by contrast, was without towns of the kind found in
Palestine in the eighth century (Brogiolo and Gelichi 1998).
With one exception – Rome.

Historians tend to be baffled by Rome. How could the great
metropolis have declined so dramatically? Yet there is incontrovertible evidence of its stupendous demise. Piranesi's etchings,
for example, free of any fancifulness, starkly convey the bewil-
dering decay of the ancient city. Similarly, Robert Macpherson's
sombre photographs taken in the 1850s of the city walls and the
Campagna Romana, the hinterland of the metropolis, depict a
catastrophe as final as those which overtook the Aztecs or
Pharaohs. The rebirth of Rome as a city after the unification of
Italy in the nineteenth century has distanced twentieth-century
generations from the extraordinary, if vexing, panoramas that
attracted grand tourists. Ancient Rome, as countless excava-

tions now attest, grew phenomenally in line with the expansion of its empire in the late Republic and early Empire, then foundered, and, with some respite in the later fourth and fifth centuries, fell into ruin as Ostia has. Of course, it was never wholly deserted; far from it. But the special history of the city, its phenomenal metropolitan grandeur and, above all, its status as a Christian epicentre run by pope-presidents (to quote Peter Llewellyn: 1986), meant that it sustained an importance that was no more than an eccentric yardstick against which we can measure the birth of medieval Europe.

Richard Krautheimer (1980) sketched the bare bones of this special history: 'Its lingering Byzantine connections in the later seventh and earlier half of the eighth centuries. Several small-scale but exquisite churches and renovations belong to this age: to an invasion of Rome by Byzantine contemporary art ... transposed into a local dialect' (1980: 99). Krautheimer had in mind the mid-seventh-century mosaics in San Stefano Rotondo depicting saints, like those of Santa Agnese fuori le mura, their heads defined using a linear system, and solidly modelled in fleshy colours. From the brief but active age of Pope John VII (705-7) there is a magnificent cycle of paintings in Santa Maria Antiqua, in the heart of the Roman Forum. Here, in Krautheimer's opinion, the 'links to Byzantium startle the eye' although the impressionism and illusionism of the rendering is supported, in contrast to the earlier Hellenistic wave, by a strong framework of black lines. Such works underscore Pope Gregory II's warning to the Byzantine Empire in 729 that 'the whole West has its eyes on us ... and on Saint Peter ... whom all the kingdoms of the West honour. We are going to the most distant parts of the West to seek those who desire baptism ... [but] their princes wish to receive from ourselves alone' (Krautheimer 1980: 106). This age has now been unearthed in two telling places.

In the esedra of the Crypta Balbi (in the Campus Martius), a remarkable excavation led initially by Daniele Manacorda, then by Lucia Saguì, has produced an invaluable sequence (Manacorda and Saguì 1995; Saguì 1993; 1998a). The abandoned esedra served first as a glass-maker's workshop in the fifth and sixth centuries. During the seventh and eighth centuries the confined space was filled with a thick deposit of rubbish from the adjoining church of San Salvatore in Pensilis. Among the many objects were lead moulds for bronze crosses and plaques, clearly used not only by the monastery's community and visiting pilgrims, but also by some of the Lombards buried in the seventh-century cemetery at Nocera Umbra in Umbria, 150 km north of Rome (Ricci 1997). On this incontrovertible evidence, liturgical objects were being manufactured by monastic craftsmen for restricted exchange purposes between the papal city and its Lombard neighbours. By the late seventh century, with the dramatic reduction of commodity production noted above, one feature of the midden stands out. The pottery assemblage contains a small number of Sicilian transport amphorae and crude but serviceable Sicilian oil lamps – indices, like the moulds, of a specific connection, this time with Byzantine production centres on Sicilian estates (Saguì, Ricci and Romei 1997). But the poverty of the economic system is most vividly illustrated by the coins in circulation at the time. These are wafer-thin bronze and poor quality silver nummi, which occur in surprising numbers in the layers within the midden (Rovelli 1998). Numismatists interpret these crude objects as a low value coinage used by Rome's impoverished aristocracy within the confines of the papal state, possibly, according to Paolo Delogu, during ceremonial occasions such as the adventus of magistrates, or the enthroning of popes. Spectrographic analysis of a hoard of similar coins (found in the Tiber in 1982) shows that the coins minted in the later seventh century had a silver content that exceeded 75%; those from the first quarter of the eighth century tended to be much poorer, while those of the mid-eighth century, the papacy of Pope Stephen II, fell to below 30% silver. The pattern is replicated by the state's high-value coins. Using similar spectrographic methods, Oddy has charted the decline of the gold content in Byzantine and Italian solidi between *c.* 640 and 760. The gold coins of the Emperor Constans II contained in excess of 90%; by 720, the Emperor Leo III's solidi contained little more than 50% gold; by 760, gold coins in Italy and Byzantium had been thoroughly debased and contained no more than 10% gold (Oddy 1988; also Oddy 1972; 1974). However challenging to historians familiar with written sources, this pattern is repeated in many other material forms. Walking down the recently excavated eighth-century phase of the Via Argileto, once one of the great streets of ancient Rome, one cannot deny the spirit of the place. The paved road, passing by the Forum of Nerva, had become a track surfaced with broken tile and rubble. Next to it, towards the end of the eighth century a small palace complex was erected. Its massing and detailing were modest beside the huge ruins of the Temple of Saturn close by, denuded of its marble to serve new churches (Santangeli Valenzani 1997; Brogiolo and Gelichi 1998). The written sources, however voluminous, cannot distract us from the real measure of these times.

Yet Rome in the first half of the eighth century cannot have been less than fascinating to the doughty Anglo-Saxon and Frankish pilgrims. The sea of ruins dwarfing the small, dispersed communities must have made an amazing sight. Moreover, taken together, these dispersed communities amounted to a sizeable population by the standards of the time. The city's population, of course, is a matter for debate and speculation. Krautheimer estimated 30-40,000 (1980: 291-2), perhaps a tenth of the city's population in the fifth century. But this may be too high. The fifty-odd ecclesiastical monuments (churches, diaconiae and monasteries) mentioned by Krautheimer would each have housed no more than 50-100 persons, given our present knowledge of the archaeology of these places. This would indicate a population of 5,000 at most – the size of a new town such as Hamwic or Dorestad on the shores of the North Sea (see Chapter 3 below). Working from another angle, Pertusi has calculated that at the end of the seventh century no more than 1200-1600 soldiers were available to defend the city (1968, 682) – a force comparable to a medium-sized West Saxon town in the Viking age. In other words, a figure of 5,000 may be closer to the mark than Krautheimer's estimate. The staggering depopulation still surprises us, but nevertheless, unlike innumerable other great classical cities now occupied by 'squatters' and a handful of families, by the standards of the age Rome was actually a great centre of population!

The archaeology of the city, however, clearly shows that Rome was awakened with Charlemagne's visit at Easter 774. As Krautheimer colourfully puts it: 'the hundred years from 760 and 860 have strongly moulded both the map of Rome and her image in contemporary thought' (1980: 109); 'for the first time in all her history, she [Rome] wants to be seen in a European, and no longer in a Mediterranean, perspective; even so, within the overall picture of the Carolingian Renascence, Rome carries a note of her own' (1980: 122-3).

Recent excavations in Santa Susanna have brought to light the paintings from one wall. The strongly defined faces of the line of saints initially puzzled art historians in Rome. The artist belonged to the short interval between the cessation of Byzantine contact in the middle of the century, and the powerful impact of the Carolingians upon the city's culture. That impact took a variety of forms. For example, Walcharius, archbishop of Sens, apparently an engineer, was despatched to Rome as a consultant to Pope Hadrian I. The result, listed in the *Liber Pontificalis*, was the refurbishment of many churches, and a staggering influx of precious gifts, notably gold and silver

(Delogu 1988; 1998b). The new churches made use of the ample quantities of Roman *spolia*, harking back to an imperial past, while the artists developed a distinctive Roman style of painting. Alongside the painters were sculptors who produced carved church furniture in marble and travertine, altar screens and panels, not only for the churches in the city but also for the numerous new foundations built on the estates in the Campagna Romana, the hinterland of the papal city. This concerted effort to promote a new ideology is reflected in the secular culture. The small palatial complex recently excavated beside the Via Argileto in the Forum of Nerva is graced by a portico and deployed *spolia* as prominently as any church (Coates-Stephens 1997; Menegnini and Santangeli Valenzani 1996).

Once again the rubbish middens found in the excavations of the esedra of the Crypta Balbi reveal the changing rhythms of the age (Saguì 1993). Byzantine amphorae and lamps are absent; instead, a small number of soapstone jars made in northern Italy are present, modest indicators of Rome's new alliance (Saguì, Ricci and Romei 1997). Significantly, though, besides the local tablewares and glasswares, the arrival of a distinctive Roman glazed ware, known as Forum ware, is most noteworthy. Forum ware pitchers have a thick olive-green lead glaze, and invariably the body of the vessel is decorated with relief petals reminiscent of the most baroque experimentation by ancient Roman potters. The investment in the Church and material life of the city went hand in hand with a pronounced revival of estates in its hinterland.

Many archaeological excavations now attest to the creation of new churches in the late eighth century on a ring of lands around Rome. Of these excavations, the Mola di Monte Gelato is the most illustrative of the new age (Potter and King 1997). The early Roman villa, refurbished in late antiquity, deserted by the seventh century, was transformed after nearly two hundred years of abandonment in the late eighth century into a minor estate church. As in Rome itself, Roman *spolia* as well as newly carved church furniture were deployed to establish the contemporary ideology. The iconography reinforced the central place of the liturgy in daily life. The popular involvement with the new liturgical drama was an essential feature of the transition. Subsumed within this drama was the basis of a new social order, the concept of servitude. Beside the little church a potter set up his kiln, producing domestic wares comparable in many ways to those found in the middens in the Crypta Balbi. As in the case of many estate churches, the peasantry almost certainly occupied modest dwellings dotted around the vicinity.

Rome clearly capitalised upon its new alliance and its perceived European importance. Flushed with Carolingian support, early in the ninth century Pope Paschal I (817-24), as the *Liber Pontificalis* attests, invested in the construction of monumental churches such as SS Quattro Coronati. The city's acquisition of huge amounts of gold and silver permitted its pope-presidents to restore it as a capital. Pinpointing the precise source of Rome's newly found opulence is a matter for speculation. Were the gold and silver hoards owned by Rome's cautious popes and aristocrats now opened? Was the city somehow able to acquire some of the later eighth-century Arabic silver, mined under Abbasid supervision in the Hindu Kush, occurring in large quantities in the Aghlabid caliphate of North Africa? Or did the Carolingians, in their desire for imperial connections, furnish the eternal city with precious metals in the form of gifts and donations (from the captured Avar treasure?) as well as technical consultants like Walcharius? The question cannot be answered (Delogu 1998b). However, the archaeological evidence suggests that the city and its estate-holders, in its startling recovery after 770 under Pope Hadrian I, certainly paid more than lip service to Carolingian ideology, but had access to a measure of the gold and silver mountains that the caliphs were currently enjoying . This was one place in

Latin Christendom that bore comparison with Constantinople and Baghdad. Its grandiosity, given its special place in the Italian peninsula, and indeed in western Europe, cannot have failed to make an impression on all who saw it.

Towns in ninth-century Italy

This great and famous city is pre-eminent in Italy
in the area of the Veneto, as Isidore teaches,
and it has been called Verona since time out of mind.

It forms a square, its walls are strongly built,
forty-eight towers in a circuit brilliantly gleam,
and eight lofty ones among them are taller than all the
  others.

It has a wide and spacious forum paved with stones,
at each of its four angles stands a great arch,
and its streets are wondrously laid with flagstones.

This anonymous ninth-century poem, the *Versus de Verona*, was written in praise of the city where the court of Pippin, Charlemagne's son and king of Italy, had settled in 799. 'Civic pride mingles with religious reservations in the poem's account of pagan antiquity's contribution to the noble reputation of Verona' (Godman 1985: 30, 181). The poem at face value lends confidence to the 'optimists' who have interpreted a continuity of townlife in Italy's Lombard towns based primarily upon the continuity of use of Roman street grids in towns such as Lucca and Verona (Ward-Perkins 1988; 1997). More probably it is an example of the impetus given to the Lombard economy following the conquest of the region by the Carolingians.

Yet the impact of the Carolingians on later eighth-century Italian townlife is not yet apparent (*pace* the 'optimist' Ward-

Perkins 1997). Indeed, of all the archaeological discoveries in Italian towns one phenomenon continues to be described in English as though it belongs to another culture: 'dark earth'. Less than twenty years ago it was unthinkable that Italian towns had simply declined and disappeared like their north European counterparts, only to re-appear in the tenth and eleventh centuries (Ward-Perkins 1988). Now, confirmed by Brogiolo and Gelichi (1998), there is no doubting that by the seventh century places such as Brescia, Milan, Naples, Otranto, Pescara and Verona were reduced to non-urban proportions rather similar to the Anatolian cities described above. The accumulation of evidence is now persuasive. Each of these places enjoyed a revival of some kind in late antiquity. Naples, like Rome, for example, flourished in the fifth century, playing a major part in western Mediterranean seaboard trade as well as participating in trade between Sicily and Rome. Likewise, excavations in Otranto, Pescara, Ravenna and Venice reveal the vigour of the Adriatic-borne trade up to the later sixth century. Dockside sprawl at Otranto, new shops at Pescara, and new dock installations at Classe – the port of Ravenna – illustrate continued investment on a significant scale. Similarly at Venice on the island of Castello, a substantial later sixth- or early seventh-century building has been uncovered, constructed on a well-made platform of timber planks, associated with which are three Byzantine imperial stamps and a gold tremissis of Emperor Heraclius I (610-41). Inland, large and small towns profited from the Mediterranean economy. Brescia, for example, the scene of two decades of major archaeological investigations, bears witness to dense continued occupation even during the later sixth and early seventh centuries when the city fell into Lombard hands. At the site of Santa Giulia in Brescia, an area once occupied by a major Roman *domus* was transformed by the city's new Lombard occupants. Up to ten buildings covering between 39m^2 and 67m^2 were constructed. The new occupants deployed post-built construction to support thatched roofs, but made expedient use of existing walls which were patched with clay. Like the so-called 'squatters' of Butrint or Cherchel described above, the architecture of Brescia's new inhabitants involved minimal investment in materials. Similar buildings were discovered in the excavations of the Forum at Luni, the Tyrhennian port which had prospered from the export of local Carrara marble.

The written sources describe other acts of expediency which, given the archaeological evidence, seem highly plausible. In the Latium hill town of Rieti, for example, the Roman-period towered dwellings were repaired and inhabited. Presumably, as in the theatre of Verona where excavations revealed makeshift buildings constructed of rubble and *spolia* poorly cemented together, the Rieti dwellings were patched structures rather than grand new buildings. Historians may question the validity of the archaeological sample. Nevertheless it has to be empha-sised that in the hundreds of trenches excavated in towns throughout Italy the commonest, if most prosaic discovery, is not the remains of buildings but 'dark earth'. This is the hall-mark of the transformation of the Roman world.

As in many parts of Rome, however, the era of 'dark earth' ended in the ninth century. In Venice the revival almost certainly dates to the years when the body of St Mark was mischievously stolen in Egypt and dedicated to the port's new cathedral. Close by St Mark's, excavations in the church of San Lorenzo have shown how it was constructed on a massive raft of sawn timbers, while out in the lagoon trial excavations on the island of San Lorenzo have revealed a sequence of late Roman graves, covered by timber buildings, covered in turn by a well-made ninth-century basilica (Brogiolo and Gelichi 1998).

The archaeological evidence of ninth-century Venice amounts to vignettes, by comparison with Rome, but it is likely to illustrate the beginnings of the port as an entrepot at the

61

head of the Adriatic sea effectively replacing Marseille as the main Mediterranean gateway into central Europe. The exceptional significance of Venice, as Henri Pirenne recognised (see Chapter 1 above) is perhaps illustrated by Charlemagne's persistent attempts to conquer the archipelago, beginning in the 780s and ending in 810 with a treaty. More telling, perhaps, is its subsequent numismatic history. Within a decade of the treaty with Charlemagne, its coins, along with other north Italian deniers, had acquired considerable status north of the Alps. According to Simon Coupland, as a recession began to hit the North Sea commercial network in the 820s (Chapters 3 and 4 below), the circulation of Italian coins north of the Alps became commoner. Coupland shows that Venetian coins (195 deniers) represented 25% of the Apremont hoard of *c.* AD 822, while coins minted in Milan and Pavia represented a further 11% of the total. Similarly, in the Belvezet hoard of the same period, 28% of the coins were from north Italian mints. A generation later, in AD 849, Abbot Lupus of Ferrieres reported that the impoverished West Frankish currency was not acceptable in Italy, only *Italica moneta argento* (Coupland 1990).

The revival of Venice and indeed of the towns of the Po valley might be ascribed as much to the re-awakening of Byzantine investment in the western Balkans in the early ninth century, as to Carolingian investment. Venice, after all, had traditional connections with the Byzantine world. Other Adriatic ports attracted new investment at least by the later decades of the century: Comacchio at the estuarine mouth of the Po may have prospered at this time (Balzaretti 1995); at Pescara a line of workshops set behind the seafront was recently discovered, modestly reminiscent of the Frisian beachside emporium at Medemblik (Staffa 1991; Besteman 1990). The workshops appear similar in size to those found at the Beneventan monastery of San Vincenzo al Volturno (see below) and, in tenth-century contexts, at Ferrara (Hodges 1997). Further south, excavations at the Byzantine naval base of Otranto in the heel of Italy attest to its revival at this time. Similar evidence in Naples and Salerno shows that the modest rebirth of towns was not restricted to the Adriatic sea region. The first links between the Beneventan ports, Byzantium, Sicily and Aghlabid North Africa provided new vigour to these places. Yet the scale of the revival should not be exaggerated. Naples, for example, according to descriptions of the town in the tenth century, was hardly built up.

The evidence is hardly conclusive, it has to be admitted. Two further discoveries, however, need to be mentioned. First, at San Vincenzo al Volturno, and in all probability at many monasteries in Italy after *c*. AD 790, with explicit if modest Carolingian support, new workshops were constructed. Initially materials such as tiles and glass were made for use in the burgeoning monastic city. Soon, however, dedicated workshops replaced the temporary ones, making enamels, ivories, glassware and probably ceramics not only for the monastery, but for its estates as well (Hodges 1997). The significant aspect of these discoveries, unlike those at the Crypta Balbi, is the technology of production and distribution. The tile kiln is paralleled in a type found in the Byzantine colonies in the Crimea; the bronze-making kiln is best paralleled by a discovery at Merv on the Silk route; the glass kiln is almost certainly a Syrian model; and the enamels followed a Byzantine tradition; the many tons of marble sculpture imported to the site as *spolia*, robbed from classical buildings, necessitated a transport system capable of meeting the monastery's wish to ornament its principal building with Roman-period columns, inscriptions and capitals (Hodges and Moran 2000). Arab objects are rare at San Vincenzo, yet just as the Abbasids were blending Graeco-Roman and Islamic concepts in town-building, so there is a hint, at least, that the artisans of this ambitious monastery were bringing together a range of ideas to help their development. Evidently, this went hand-in-hand with increased rural production on the monastery's estates, leading to a *vicus* being created outside its precinct by the 820s. Secondly, with the articulation of the great monastic estates, as in France (Devroey 1993; Toubert 1983), there was a need for new market-places – and if these did not exist, they were created. Notable examples of these new mid-ninth-century towns are Sicopolis near Capua and Centocelle near Civitavecchia (Marazzi 1994). As yet, apart from the Leonine city in Rome, these places are barely known. Yet, distinguished by their walls and public buildings, these were evident attempts to develop regional economies based on the concept of townlife.

Conclusion

Pirenne believed that the Mediterranean economy died and, as a result, this region became separated from north-west Europe. The extraordinary demise of classical antiquity cannot be over-stated. Yet in places like Rome, Constantinople and the Levant, classical notions of urbanism and, especially, production, persisted. Everything was on a reduced scale, yet this conti-nuity almost certainly represented a significant link between the world of antiquity and the age of Charlemagne. It was a link that was not lost on the great Carolingian leader. In this sense the connection of Mohammed and Charlemagne in Pirenne's celebrated hypothesis may not be farfetched. One final example illustrates this entangled history of Carolingian energy and Mediterranean ideas. It is an illustration, as we shall see in the following chapters, that has a bearing on the making of medieval towns north of the Alps.

One of the most important written sources illustrating Carolingian trade is a letter despatched by Charlemagne to King Offa of Mercia, shortly after the death of Pope Hadrian I in AD 796. The letter discusses the problems of merchants illicitly posing as pilgrims to evade paying customs tolls and stresses the need to give merchants the support of the law. The letter then replies to a request made by King Offa in an earlier letter:

> As for the black stones which your Reverence begged to be sent to you, if a messenger comes and considers what kind you have in mind, we will willingly order for them to be given, wherever they are to be found, and will help with their transport. But as you have intimated your wishes concerning the length of the stones, so our people make a demand about the size of cloaks, that you may order them to be such as used to come to us in former times. (Whitelock 1955: 782)

What were the black stones? Many scholars have interpreted them as millstones made of Mayen lava (Hodges 1982: 124) – millstones which were extremely popular in Roman as well as later medieval times. Charlemagne's interest was perhaps captured by the fact that the Mayen quarries were located close to the Rhine valley, only about 100 km from his palace at Aachen. Yet, in a fascinating reassessment, D.P.S. Peacock has questioned the interpretation of this letter: would Charlemagne have troubled himself with something as basic as a humble millstone (1997)? And if so, why the reference to their length, when millstones were quantified by their diameter or number? Moreover, the tenor of the text is that these black stones were not a regular item of trade to be entrusted to merchants, but probably more of a gift of considerable significance. Peacock offers an alternative interpretation: these were porphyry columns.

Recalling the description by Einhard, Charlemagne's biographer, of the removal of marbles from Ravenna and Rome for his palaces and churches, Peacock proceeds to show that the most treasured of columns – befitting a personal letter between two of the most powerful men in the western world, were those of black porphyry. Red porphyry was obtained from Mons Porphyrites in the eastern desert of Egypt. The Byzantine monarchs adopted it as their own, calling it the 'Roman stone', partly because their supplies came as *spolia* from Rome and partly because they regarded themselves as Romans. Porphyry was extremely rare north of the Alps. There is some in a small portable altar from Adelhausen, and from the 850s, a porphyry plaque from Ravenna which according to one source was 'exceedingly valuable and very translucent, like glass' (Greenhalgh 1989: 132). Black porphyry was even rarer: only the palace cathedral of Aachen has columns made of this marble. Among the status-conscious royalty of the later eighth century, these must have been the object of great admiration and a symbol of domination. The rarity of the stone, however, may explain Charlemagne's prevarication: 'send a messenger with more precise details and we will look around to see what can be found', he replied.

The new cathedral at Aachen, resplendant with *spolia* brought from Ravenna as well as its 'black stones', remains a symbolic monument to the Carolingian renaissance which, according to the French architectural historian Carol Heitz, encompassed the building of 27 new cathedrals, 417 monasteries and 100 royal palaces, most within the Rhine-Seine region (Heitz 1980). It is not difficult to appreciate King Offa's admiration for this stone as well as his willingness to trade woollen cloaks to play a part in the making of this new cultural order. The emperor of the English, as he titled himself on occasions, was as attracted to imperial glory as his continental peer, Charlemagne. He too might make use of Graeco-Roman symbolism in advancing his political supremacy. Yet the basis of this wealth evidently did not come from either Rome itself or the Mediterranean. Quite clearly, as we have seen in this

2. Charlemagne's elephant

chapter, Italy, as much as it owed to Arab and Byzantine connections from the late eighth century, was in most matters in thrall to the Carolingians who provided the impetus for economic as well as cultural transformation.

3

Dream cities – non-places

Cities have often been likened to symphonies and poems;
and this comparison seems to me a perfectly natural one:
they are in fact objects of the same nature ... something
lived and something dreamed. (Levi-Strauss 1989: 115).

A historiography of Dark Age non-places

Dark Age emporia, in their time, must have seemed 'something
lived ... something dreamed'. As one sailed into these ports,
there must have been an intense sense of buzzing activity, and,
above all, an extraordinary number of people. In a world that
was essentially under-populated, visitors must have marvelled
at these places. They were the binary opposite of what Jacques
Le Goff terms the desert-forest phenomenon – the remote
places where holy men introduced the concept of natural order
to realise their dreams about the city of God (Le Goff 1988). Not
until the end of the millennium, as the urban phenomenon
became more natural to Europe, do we find written descriptions
of emporia. Herein lies an interesting problem for the historian:
archaeology has unearthed a major political, demographic and
economic element in early medieval society, the importance of
which transcends the simple question of daily living.

This class of settlement is a special phenomenon because it is
virtually an archaeological contribution to history. For this
reason it needs to be defined with some care. Emporia were

gateway communities, funnelling monopolistically-controlled regional and inter-regional exchange. The economic and geographical bases of the system of which they formed a part were very different from those in place in antiquity, and equally different from the high and later medieval systems of regional, competitive markets with their spaces defined, as Sennett has noted, by Christian ritual (1994). The huge body of archaeological evidence now shows that these places were noticeably lacking in ritual components, in stark contrast to the late classical notions of Augustine's City of God. These were places motivated by the economic, driven by the stomach, to quote the twelfth-century philosopher, John of Salisbury. In short, these emporia were neither the consumer cities of classical antiquity (Finley 1981; Veyne 1990), nor pre-capitalist marketplaces such as occur in the later Middle Ages. It is simplest to describe them as products of kin-based societies in which the division of labour was, perhaps surprisingly, still in an embryonic state. Their history belongs to the period in which the division of labour was actively taking shape, and spans the time until exchange was first transacted in society by a market mechanism. This class of settlement, therefore, may lie beyond the historian's horizon, yet it is a manifestation of a critical moment in the formation of post-classical Europe.

As such, to use Marc Augé's term, these were non-places (1998). It is not far-fetched to regard them as technical solutions to urbanism, often criticised as places to live because they fail to produce an older, slower history (Augé 1998: 66). Fundamentally, these were places lacking monuments and unfitted to breeding a sense of either the sacred or history and memory.

Modern history begins in the age of emporia. The ancient mode of production had been superseded by what might be termed a medieval one (Wickham 1984; Mann 1986). The transition in economic terms seems to have been much more complex than has hitherto been imagined. It is likely, therefore, that European society lived betwixt and between one mode and the other for many generations – trapped in the traumatic problems of change. Nevertheless, the roots of the spirit of capitalism, it might be argued, are to be found in the spirit behind the making of the emporia. Inevitably, such issues bring to mind the historiographic contributions of such influential social thinkers as Karl Marx and Max Weber.

A century ago problems of nationalism and materialism were no less thought-provoking than they are today. These, as Anthony Giddens has shown, proved the setting for several studies about the origins of the western economy (1971). The most familiar thesis is the Marxian contribution. It is a deterministic thesis founded upon the struggle between the classes, and to a lesser extent control of technology. The essence of this thesis focuses upon the formation of feudal societies, arising from the synthesis of Roman and Germanic societies. In Marx's view, only the collapse of feudal society and the concomitant growth of urban centres, coupled with new ethnological breakthroughs and the discovery of rich overseas territories, produced the favourable conditions for a capitalist economy (Giddens 1971). Max Weber, writing at the turn of the century, a generation after Marx, believed that these transformations, as important as they might be, could not explain the typical capitalist mentality. A mentality of devoted and morally purposive work, wealth-producing for the sake of economic aggrandisement and perpetual reinvestment, could not be explained as a natural outcome of either greedy capitalism or new economic developments. The traditional dominant orientation toward work, according to Weber, has been characterised by the attempt by the very many to maintain standards of living, or by the very few to accumulate in order to spend on luxury goods (Giddens 1971; Mann 1986). Thus he showed how difficult it was in a traditional atmosphere to stimulate in a time of need a motivation toward higher productivity. Weber argued that

71

modern capitalism involved a spirit that gave to it a moral purpose which could be contrasted with that of traditionalism.

This spirit was traced by Weber to Protestant thinking and teaching; the first beginnings, though, he seeks in Christian asceticism. In arguably his most famous book, *The Protestant Ethic and the Spirit of Capitalism* (1907), he writes: 'Without doubt Christian asceticism, both outwardly and in its inner meaning, contains many different things. But it has had a definitely rational character .... The great historical significance of Western monasticism, as contrasted with that of the Orient, is based on this fact .... In the rules of St Benedict, again with the Cistercians, and most strongly the Jesuits, it has become emancipated from planless otherworldliness and irrational self torture. It has developed a systematic method of rational conduct with the purpose of overcoming the status naturae, to free man from the power of irrational impulses and his dependence on the world and on nature' (Weber 1989: 118-19).

Weber was not alone in examining what he saw as the rational evolution of the European post-classical economy. For example, shortly before Weber's treatise on the protestant ethic appeared, Werner Sombart published *Der moderne Kapitalismus* (1902), a study which focussed upon demand in luxury goods rather than trade as the motor pushing the development of mercantile, industrial and finance capital (Sombart 1902: 131ff.; Parsons 1928). Sombart argued that 'the stream of commodities which enters and leaves a (medieval) town would not support a single sparrow'. In Sombart's opinion the town was made of political leaders (kings, lay and ecclesiastical lords) who controlled revenues derived from the countryside around about, or the taxes from the region. It was these leaders who attracted and patronised craftsmen who in turn patronised shopkeepers. This demand, Sombart concluded, generated the need for trade. Finley, writing of ancient cities, has called this the consumer city (1981; Veyne 1990).

3. Dream cities – non-places

The First World War separates these great theorists from the historical studies which have set the agenda for twentieth-century historiography. Marc Bloch (and the French historians known collectively as the Annales school), much influenced by Pirenne, constructed a model for the evolution of Latin Christendom founded upon feudalism (Fink 1989). Its starting-point owes more than a little to Marx. The rational explanations of Sombart and Weber were largely overlooked (Veyne 1990: 37, and Mann 1986 respectively). Woven into this feudal model was Pirenne's thesis, born of the combination of his historical research into Flemish towns and his searing experiences in a German prisoner-of-war camp (Lyon 1974). Pirenne's thesis, as we have already seen, has been much discussed. Essentially it runs counter to Sombart's interpretation of the medieval town: medieval towns, according to Pirenne, 'were the work of merchants: they existed only for them' (1895: 70). Medieval towns, he argued, were nurtured by the feudal orders of Latin Christendom and belong to the aftermath of the Carolingian age, once the socio-economic scaffolding of Europe had been erected (see Chapter 1 above).

After the Second World War the shadow of Pirenne drove many historians towards new fields of enquiry. Neo-marxian thinking has been principally concerned with man's longer-term place in history, fashioned in particular by Fernand Braudel, and in recent times with the structural history of mentalities (Braudel 1977). Two leading exponents illustrate the point: Georges Duby and Jacques Le Goff were initially historians of *la longue durée*, and now, with creative imagination, are reconstructing the structural concepts of medieval society. For them, as Levi-Strauss put it, the city is quintessentially something lived and something dreamed. Fundamentally, though, Pirenne's thesis still props up the history of towns in Latin Christendom (Duby 1974; Le Goff 1980). This is quite understandable: few new written sources have been found to

73

shed light on the Pirenne thesis. Only archaeology offers some new means of interrogating the few witnesses of this formative age.

Archaeologists, it has to be confessed, have been slow to become involved in this great debate. In fact, the history of excavations in emporia stands far apart from the broad current of European historiography. Hjalmar Stolpe was excavating at Birka, the Viking-period site in middle Sweden, while Marx was still alive (Hyenstrand 1992). His discoveries purport to show that beyond the bounds of Latin Christendom, in the very heart of pagan Scandinavia, lay a merchant's town of great importance. This scarcely squared with Marx's model, let alone Marc Bloch's concept of Europe. Holger Arbman, who eventually published Stolpe's remarkable work in 1940-43, fashioned the arguments in his *Schweden und das karolingischer Reich* (1937). The imposing menace of Nazi Germany doubtless contributed to Arbman's thinking. A more substantive influence, however, was the powerful tradition of liberal post-First World War German historiography with its great emphasis upon the revival of classical imperialism under German hegemony – the Carolingian renaissance. Erwin Panofsky, Richard Krautheimer and, a little later, Walter Ullmann, to name only three, were actively shaping a model of Carolingian dominance which owed much to their understanding of late antiquity as well as early medieval texts. Not unnaturally, Arbman concluded that Sweden, and Birka in particular, were nurtured by proximity to Charlemagne's empire. Put another way, Christian mercantilism, much as Max Weber saw it, was a powerful, rational force in shaping this pagan history. At face value Arbman was pinpointing the origins of towns and trade – giving some flesh to the skeleton outlined in Pirenne's thesis. Arbman's research drew upon discoveries made in the preceding twenty years at two other emporia: Dorestad (situated at the confluence of the rivers Lek and Rhine in the

3. Dream cities – non-places

Netherlands) and Haithabu (Hedeby, near Schleswig at the base of Jutland).

J.H. Holwerda, who excavated at Dorestad in the 1920s, revealed the wealth of data pertaining to commerce in the Dark Ages awaiting discovery in this Frisian emporium (1930). Like the story of Birka, it was a history at odds with the Christian vision of European history, yet one that might be readily explained by it. Finally, at the very time that Arbman was writing his book, large excavations were being made at Haithabu, the Danish emporium at the foot of Jutland. Here, the young Herbert Jankuhn, working with SS support, was undoubtedly taking his quest for the origins of German imperial mercantilism (he actually calls it the German Reich in his article published in the Cambridge-based journal, *Antiquity*, in 1939) in the Carolingian age to dangerous extremes (Arnold 1990). Jankuhn was forcing the historiographic frontiers. Pirenne's thesis was fashioned into a simple formula: long-distance trade gave birth to towns which in turn fed the feudal powers of Latin Christendom.

Post-war excavations of emporia, like those of medieval towns, have mostly taken place beyond the immediate bounds of mainstream historiography. Excavations in Hamwih (now known as Hamwic, or Anglo-Saxon Southampton) began in 1946 (Morton 1992), like those in Ipswich, London (Lundenwic and Lundenburg) and York (Eoforwic and Jorvik), in order to construct a town history. Local history lay behind this research. Herein lay what Marc Bloch termed the dangerous idol of origins (Bloch 1954: 31). This phase of data collection, to be fair, must be paralleled with the patient publication of the printed chronicles and texts in the *Monumenta Germaniae Historica* a century before, which made it possible for Marx and Weber, as well as Pirenne and Bloch, for example, to shape major theses about the evolution of Europe. As the archaeologists unearthed their chronicles, however, it was inevitable that they should search for an overarching model to explain these unusually rich

75

places. Not surprisingly, the history of excavations of emporia such as Southampton (Hamwic), London (Lundenwic), Ipswich, York (Eoforwic), Dorestad, Medemblik, Ribe, Arhus and Kaupang (Hodges 1982) has been shaped by a Carolingian mercantile perspective introduced by Arbman and Jankuhn half a century ago. This thesis, it might be said, found its ultimate, if perhaps unlikely, conclusion in my book *Dark Age Economics* (1982). This book, as many reviewers recognised, was written under the influence of Colin Renfrew's studies of prehistoric trade (e.g. Renfrew 1975), and Marshall Sahlins' studies of the conditions of pre-market exchange (e.g. Sahlins 1974). But the archaeology of the emporia, of course, did not end there! During the 1980s and 1990s the scale of archaeological research greatly increased, and the economics of the emporia have begun to look very different (Hodges 1989). The database offers a challenge not only to the twentieth-century models of living in these cities, but also, perhaps, to how they featured in dreams.

Open-area excavations and the apparatus of modern archaeology provide the opportunity to step beyond the extant historiography (see, for example, studies such as Andrews 1997; van Es 1990 and the astute historical re-reading of these archaeological reports by Stéphane Lebecq). The huge scale of the excavations, beginning with van Es' remarkable decision to uncover a great swathe of the riverside settlement at Dorestad during the 1960s and 1970s, makes it possible to discuss the concept of urban planning (van Es 1990; Hodges 1999). Similarly, the scientific analysis of the colossal body of finds from these places, ranging from craft debris to food refuse, reveals most convincingly how they functioned.

Chronological parameters: North Sea emporia *c.* 600-850

The spirit, even the practice, of a pre-capitalist economy begins to emerge. Without any doubt, dark age economics were

founded on complex principles. To define these principles we
need to fix ourselves in time and place – in archaeological time-
slices.

From the later sixth century to c. 675 The first time-slice
belongs to the later sixth century and spans the period up to
about 675. This is the moment when the Mediterranean
economy was virtually extinguished (see Chapter 2 above).
More specifically, what I have termed type A emporia – essentially administered *periodic* market-places – belong to the
re-formation of the Merovingian North Sea in the last quarter
of the sixth century (Wood 1994). In the first instance, these
places are almost certainly an expression of Merovingian lords
pushing for control of prestige goods with which to enlarge
their coercive authority over land and labour. The type A settlement at many excavated emporia has remained elusive. In
comparison to the type B settlements discussed below, these
first fairs and periodic markets were ephemeral in structural
terms. Many were perhaps no more than tent-like structures,
erected for short seasons. Perhaps the best illustration has been
found at Ipswich. Remains of a small riverside settlement have
come to light on the north side of the river Gipping. This existed
at the time that the Sutton Hoo cemetery was being used.
Rhenish and Frankish Merovingian imported tablewares occur
in significant numbers along with pre-Ipswich ware forms
(Wade 1988). This place, we must imagine, was the gateway
community through which came much of the Frankish material
interred at Sutton Hoo. Only later, probably at the very end of
the eighth century, was it transformed into a large type B settlement with a grid of streets and quarters for artisans.

From c. 675 to between 775 and 790 The second time-slice
begins in the 670s. At this time, it appears that Dorestad (van Es
1990) and perhaps Quentovic, situated close to the mouth of the
river Canche in northern France (Hill et al 1990; Lebecq 1993)
as well as perhaps Rouen on the river Seine (Gauthier 1989)

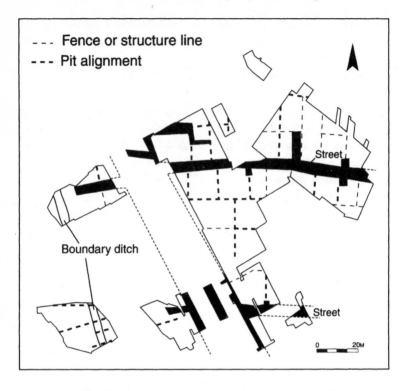

Fig. 4. The Six Dials area of (north) Hamwic showing the topography of the town *c*. 800 (after Andrews 1997).

were founded as large centres of permanent occupation. Following this, towards the end of the century there was the foundation of Hamwic (Morton 1992), London (Lundenwic) (Vince 1990), York (Eoforwic) (Kemp 1996) and Ipswich (Wade 1988), followed shortly by Medemblik (Besteman 1990) and Ribe (Bencard, Jørgensen and Madsen 1990). Smaller, subsidiary customs posts were founded in the shadow of these great centres, often taking the same topographic shape as the major emporia (e.g. Medemblik: Besteman 1990, and Norwich: Ayers

1994; see also Lebecq 1994). These are type B emporia characterised by permanent settlements often with gridded streets, and accommodation for large numbers of craftsmen. These were centres of monopolistic regional production, albeit distinctive for their involvement in long-distance trade. The fundamental characteristic of the emporia is the existence of a marked division of labour, doubtless affirmed by royal customs officials.

From c. 793/4 to c. 850. A third time-slice begins at the end of the eighth century, and spans the period up to the mid to later ninth century. This time-slice symbolically begins with the reform of the Carolingian monetary system in *c.* 793/4 (Grierson and Blackburn 1986). This period marks the final flourishing of the emporia, with increasing emphasis upon regional as opposed to inter-regional production. Nearly all these places experienced a dramatic downturn in their fortunes in the second quarter of the ninth century, leading to the desertion of most of them in favour of other nearby successor sites (see Chapter 4). Dorestad was abandoned, as was Quentovic. Hamwic was replaced by Southampton; Lundenwic was succeeded by Lundenburg; and Eoforwic was succeeded by Jorvik (see Chapter 4). Of the great North Sea emporia, only Ipswich continued to occupy the same location throughout the seventh to eleventh centuries.

The principles of non-places

What principles were fundamental to the making of these historical non-places? In the absence of any scientifically useful documentary evidence, we must turn to the archaeological record.

The type A periodic centres were essentially the foci for a ranked sphere of exchange. The idiom of these places was a trade in prestige goods. Invariably this occurred at places where boats might be readily moored or beached (Ulriksen 1994). This is scarcely at odds with the model first sketched before and after the Second World War by scholars such as Arbman and Jankuhn. However, it is hardly fully consistent with the familiar model of feudal development driven by internal competition for landed resources (Steuer 1990). The evidence for type B and, indeed, subsequent variants of this emporium, reveals altogether different foundation principles. First, these were invariably places without a previous history. Second, these were centres in which a huge, organised investment was made, almost certainly by a king or similar authority in order strategically to control the production and distribution of a region using a dedicated customs service.

More specifically, the colossal investment in the post-and-plank built wharfs at Dorestad shows that it was an entrepot, par excellence. A huge volume of trade passed through these wharfs from production centres in the Rhineland en route to places in North Germany and Jutland from *c.* 675 intermittently until the 820s. Quentovic, situated in northern France, appears to have played a slightly different role. Exploratory research at Vismarest, the putative site of Quentovic, indicates that this was a large urban centre covering more than 35 hectares with significant industrial activity (Hill et al. 1990; Lebecq 1993).

Inevitably, it is tempting to interpret the archaeological discoveries so far made at Quentovic in the light of Hamwic, Dorestad and Ribe. At Hamwic, about AD 700 (see Andrews 1997; Hinton 1996; Morton 1992), an urban settlement in excess of 40 hectares was laid out within a deep enclosure ditch. It was a new town of the kind that is familiar in the High Middle Ages, close to a small Romano-British centre, Clausentum. Hamwic's rectilinear grid of streets suggests that this was the product of an architect familiar with classical cities. (It was nearly four times the size of the Umayyad town of 'Anjar, founded in *c.* 715 on the road between Damascus and Beirut, discussed in Chapter 2.) Andrews shows that unmetalled streets were marked out before any buildings were in place in the Six Dials area (1997: 253). The plan of Hamwic, like the timber *cuneus* at the Northumbrian palace of Yeavering (Hope-Taylor 1977), the overshot water-mill at the West Saxon palace of Old Windsor (Hodges 1989: 112; Lohrmann 1989), and the earliest Anglo-Saxon churches (Morris 1989), reveals the actions of an architect who, while rational in adapting local resources to an alien idea, was as ambitious as his contemporary who built 'Anjar (Hillenbrand 1999). Still more interesting, as far as our enquiry is concerned, is the settlement matrix at Hamwic.

Unlike 'Anjar, Hamwic was not divided into quadrants with different purposes. The trading community was probably confined to the foreshore at the south end of the town. Otherwise, the pattern of occupation is essentially homogeneous. No palace or public buildings, apart from modest cemeteries and possible churches, have been found. The major excavations at the Six Dials area of the settlement, towards the northern part of the town, emphasised beyond doubt that the engine of activity was craft production on an impressive scale. Virtually all the 68 buildings were involved in interdependent multi-craft activities including various types of metal production, bone and antler working, possibly bead production, possibly pottery production, and almost certainly crafts involving perishable materials such as leather-working, carpentry, and so on (Andrews 1997). The workshops, of course, were quite unlike the familiar proto-medieval late Saxon structures in London (Vince 1990) or Anglo-Scandinavian structures excavated, for example, at Coppergate, York (Hall 1984: 49ff.). Instead, these were rural buildings adapted to the new purposes: 'despite [the absence of farm buildings], there is no evidence that Hamwic's house-forms differed from those of non-urban settlements. In this respect Six Dials, and Hamwic as a whole, may have been distinguished only by a higher

density and more regular layout of buildings and properties'
(Andrews 1997: 55). Unlike rural buildings, some were
equipped with keys and locks (as were buildings in most of the
emporia) (Hinton 1996: 50-1). This seems to illustrate the
inception of a non-tribal ethos of privacy.

Hamwic was a monopolistic centre for regional craft production as well as – and with time it appears to represent a
subsidiary activity – administered exchange in prestige goods.
Less well known, but undeniably similar in concept and development, were the new towns of Lundenwic and Eoforwic. These
were founded close to the abandoned Roman cities of London
and York, respectively. Lundenwic grew to cover 60 hectares or
more (Clark 1999); the size of Eoforwic, occupying one side of
the river Ouse, has yet to be defined, but according to Kemp it
was certainly 10 and perhaps as much as 65 hectares (Kemp
1996).

Arguably more fascinating than these sites in the Christian
heartlands are the discoveries at Ribe. This Danish emporium
was founded in the early years of the eighth century, possibly by
King Ongendus, described a generation later by Alcuin as a
man more savage than any wild beast and harder than any
stone. Again, while the traded goods and the imitation of
Dorestad's ('Wodan Monster') silver sceattas (Metcalf 1994)
initially attracted attention, it is now the evidence of urban
planning and the existence of multi-craft workshops arranged
as tenements behind a large open area which shows that the
foundation of Ribe was a signal political achievement (Bencard,
Jørgenson and Madsen 1990). Willibrord's mission to Denmark,
recounted some decades later by Alcuin, is likely to have sought
out Ongendus, the probable founder of Ribe, precisely because
of his perceived political abilities. Ongendus, prefiguring King
Godfred, the early ninth-century founder of the type B
(gridded) settlement at Haithabu (Hedeby) on the Danish frontier with the Franks, presents us with a fascinating

conundrum. It seems almost irrelevant, except of course to the missionaries, that the architect of this achievement was a pagan.

The thrust of contemporary studies suggests that the model for Ribe and its management was either Dorestad or one of the other Frisian ports. However, notwithstanding the imported Rhenish glass and pottery, it is the town's role in the regional agrarian (cattle-based) economy, possibly articulated by the silver currency, which is eye-catching. Was the Church actively involved because of its signally modest involvement in the Christian emporia in Frankia, Frisia and Anglo-Saxon England (Hodges 1982: 55-6)? Undoubtedly, as Lebecq has shown (1989: 420), the Church appreciated the economic significance of the emporia and held extensive holdings in many of them (Besteman 1990: Medemblik; van Es 1990: Dorestad).

A new order

The excavations at Ribe emphasise a point that was already clear at Southampton. The Arbman-Jankuhn model, laying emphasis upon emporia as customs and trading-stations, is misleading. The factor common to all the type B emporia is the creation of a new order – urban craftsmen – leading to social interdependence and productive specialisation which inevitably broke the ethos of a kin-based society. Craftsmen, it would appear, almost certainly outnumbered merchants (Lebecq 1999).

To be precise, the archaeology illustrates the roots of what Georges Duby has called the three orders of medieval society – knights, churchmen and workmen (1982). Simultaneously, the archaeology of these towns sheds light on the origins of the Carolingian phenomenon of the collective workshop, where many different craftsmen worked together in supervised circumstances. The collective workshop has been best known hitherto from the example depicted on the plan of St Gall of *c*. 820 (Horn and Born 1979: vol. ii, 189ff.).

The archaeology of production as opposed to trade involves examining the emporia from a very different standpoint. It is a subject, of course, that has not been ignored by historians (Ovitt 1986). In recent years the emergence of labour as a quantified entity in early medieval society has been ascribed to the Carolingian renaissance (Le Goff 1980; 1990). Duby, in his seminal book on the three orders – *oratores*, *bellatores*, and *laboratores* – adheres to the Weberian line that the creation of a structured medieval society was designed by the Benedictines during the Carolingian age. He concludes that it was a rational response to a developing, exploitative society (Andreolli and Montanari 1983: 129-45; esp. 144). Like many others (Nelson 1988), though, Duby is mystified that the first treatise on the concept of a division of labour was written by King Alfred, and occurs in his preface to the translation of Boethius' *De Consolatione Philosophiae* (Duby 1982: 99ff.; Nelson 1988; Yorke 1991). Duby overlooks the existence of the collective workshop on the schematic plan for the monastery at St Gall, dated to *c*. 820. True to Marc Bloch's thesis, Duby is concerned with agricultural labourers, not the makers of commodities. Yet in the collective workshop depicted on the St Gall plan there were *laboratores* producing arms (swords and shields) as well as other materials for the feudal elite in a monastic context. In this building the three orders intersected (Horn and Born 1979; Hodges 1997). As a concept the collective workshop appears to be a consequence of the decisions taken at the reform synods of Aachen in 816 and 817 (Horn and Born 1979: vol. ii, 189). Monasteries were no longer to be retreats in what Le Goff terms the desert-forest, but centres of civilisation promoting the spirit of an age of revival. In a sense monasteries were passing through the stages witnessed in the emporia: from type A small places of limited functional variability to type B centres controlling regions. Many monasteries, in fact, had become the legionary fortresses of the Carolingian Empire (the *kloster-politik*) – places from which the new ideology might be propagated. Control of the production of socially-important classes of commodities was a fundamental tenet of these renaissance centres (Hodges 1995).

More than a century separates the foundation of the type B emporia from the renaissance monastic cities of the early ninth century. Excavations at Hamwic and Ribe, to take two illustrations, show that as early as the eighth century there were workshops in which a variety of crafts was practised. The third order was meeting a demand, to re-state Sombart's point (1902: 131ff.), created on the estates of those who owned property in the emporia. By the end of the eighth century, this demand had risen to considerable proportions, while the trade in prestige goods may have supported little more than Sombart's proverbial sparrow. With the rise of the Carolingian ideal, though, the ethos of mercantilism revived in a new pronounced form, albeit for a short period only. It was this activity, some of it documented, that caught the eye of Henri Pirenne, as Delogu noted (1998a) (see Chapter 1). What Pirenne and Bloch, for example, were unable to identify, given the silence of the written sources about the emporia as well as the then absence of archaeological evidence, was the ever-increasing production within the emporia to meet regional demand.

This line of argument obviously begs one important question: how was the concept of type B emporia introduced to north-west Europe? Type A emporia concerned with long-distance trade had a long genesis. These places were an integral part of the exchange of prestige goods, an issue which has been much discussed (Hodges 1982). Type B emporia, on the other hand, involved a concept which was not simply the design and construction of the place, but also the will to make such a place

85

function. They embody three features which were alien to much of later seventh and early eighth-century Latin Christendom. First, the emporia were consciously transgressing the ethos of kin-based society, aggregating peoples for economic purposes (Le Goff 1980: 60). Second, the creation of collective workshops to serve and meet regional demands was at odds with the spirit of the age, and, in particular, with the Church. In late antiquity Benedict of Nursia had contended that the Church (and, with it, society) should work to be self-sufficient. Labour, if productive, should be consecrated to God (Ovitt 1986: 10-11; 16-18). Third, in much of Latin Christendom, the seats of power and authority remained at places with Roman antecedents. Kings and bishops inhabited small parts of otherwise derelict Roman towns such as Brescia, as was noted in Chapter 2. The emporia, in common with many new monasteries in the desert-forests, represented a sharp break with this Graeco-Roman/Judaeo-Christian tradition (Le Goff 1990).

What was the reason for favouring new foundations as opposed to cultivating an urban tradition extending back into classical antiquity? Hamwic was located across the river from the Roman port of Clausentum; Lundenwic was built outside the walls of the Roman city of London; Eoforwic and now, it seems, Rouen, likewise (Gauthier 1989). Dorestad lay opposite the ancient riverside fort on the *limes*. We can only speculate that in the case of the emporia the reasoning behind the choice of these new sites bore some conceptual resemblance to that of the missionaries who made new monasteries in the wilderness. In the new monasteries, holy men were seeking a paradise in the form of a pure spirituality (Le Goff 1988: 50-1). They broke away from the traditional seats of clerical power to establish a metaphysical connection with the powerful tradition of spirituality preached by St Augustine, St Benedict and other fathers of late antiquity. Le Goff summarises this in biblical terms: the wilderness

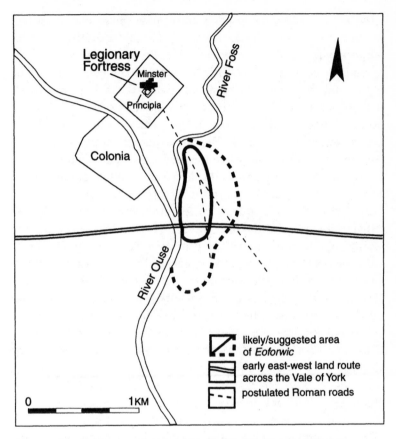

Fig. 5. The topography of Eoforwic (York) in *c*. 800 (after
Kemp 1996).

represented values opposed to the city – Seth and Cain, the
sons of Adam and Eve, fostered religion and civilisation
respectively. In the Middle Ages, Le Goff argues, the contrast
was not between the city and culture (*urbs* and *rus*, as the
Romans had put it), but between men who lived in groups and
those who lived in solitude. Monasteries, of course, might be

sited far from centres of population; new towns could not be. In particular, the ideals inherent in the planning of the emporia could not overlook the advantages of natural lines of communication. Yet it is difficult to avoid the conclusion that a rational decision was being taken by these first medieval urban planners to step outside the shadow of classical antiquity. Indeed, the new towns appear to be a medieval interpretation of (a) early Roman urban town-planning, and (b) the late Roman/early Islamic emphasis upon production in contrast to consumption. Indeed, it was in late antiquity, for a short spell only, that the productive town as opposed to the early Roman consumer city was created, serving a network of rural estates (Randsborg 1991). If the late antique or Umayyad city was indeed the prototype for the type B emporium of northern Europe, it needs to be noted that no new towns of this kind have so far been found in the Mediterranean between the seventh and beginning of the ninth centuries (see, however, Balzaretti 1995). When making the blueprints for places like Quentovic or Hamwic, or even Ribe outside Christendom, the architects must have looked elsewhere to find models for the productive activities of the settlement. The most familiar model would have been the small craft villages in the Frankish kingdoms which were diminutive forms of the sprawling (unfortified) industrial vici of the Roman age (Whittaker 1990). The best known craft villages of the Merovingian age are the potteries, notably those in the Vorgebirge Hills situated between Bonn and Cologne (Hodges 1981). We might justly deduce that if there could be villages comprising numerous potters, it seems likely that there also existed villages of smiths and glass-makers. It would be unwise to exaggerate the size of these industrial communities, and equally, in a world in which commodity production had diminished to a fraction of its Roman proportions, the status of these craftsmen should not be underestimated. It is not known who managed these craft villages, though it is likely that they formed important elements in royal and monastic estates.

Conclusion

The emporia remain an enigma because they pertain to a secular ideal, diametrically opposed to the prevailing ideals of the Church. Unlike the towns of late antiquity and the High Middle Ages, major churches were significantly absent. Paradoxically, though, the Church may have been the agency which provided the blueprints for the construction of many of these places. Holy men were the most mobile figures in Dark Age Europe (McCormick 1998). They criss-crossed Christendom following the roads made by the fabled giants of classical antiquity. Invariably, too, they stayed in guest-houses attached to the bishops' palaces in the shrunken, derelict Roman towns. In essence, their journeys took them through the ruinous towns of antiquity, leaving, we may imagine, a powerful, perhaps an indelible impression, upon these travellers. Much like modern tourists, they cannot fail to have admired the gridded streets, the market-places, the theatres and, above all, the planning of classical towns. As in modern Ostia or the coastal towns of Asia Minor or North Africa, it is these features which are memorable. Today, at least, the townhouses, by contrast, are lost in rampant vegetation. How these monkish experiences were communicated to north European kings remains a mystery. Clearly, at first, the Church was wary of the new emporia, and, in particular, their operations. Nevertheless, as Lebecq (1989) has shown, the emporia figure prominently in the saints' lives. They feature still more prominently a little later, as the Carolingian church recast its attitudes to labour. Thereafter it became ethically easier to participate, in every sense, in the emporia.

Towns and Trade in the Age of Charlemagne

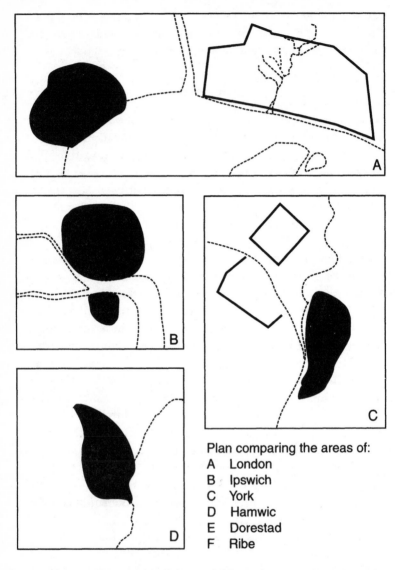

Plan comparing the areas of:
A   London
B   Ipswich
C   York
D   Hamwic
E   Dorestad
F   Ribe

Fig. 6. Comparisons of the principal towns of the eighth to ninth
centuries (after Kemp 1996).

90

3. Dream cities – non-places

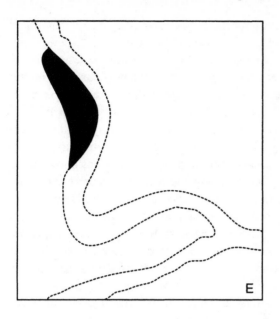

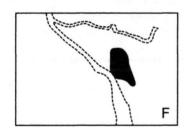

 likely / suggested line
of water course

 likely / suggested
settlement areas

 Roman defended sites

0   2 KM

One final question, pertinent to an enquiry which began with Marx, Sombart and Weber: where do the emporia belong in the making of Latin Christendom? Any answer to this question must be little more than speculation. They occur only on and beyond the fringes of Latin Christendom, where peer-polity interaction was most intense (the model discussed in Renfrew and Cherry 1986). The tribal-based rivalry between lords, and between kings, fed an appetite for change. The source of this rivalry is elusive, but is likely to have been the notions of power made in the heartlands of Merovingian and later Carolingian Europe. Long-distance trade – pre-Carolingian mercantilism – extending out beyond the feudal powers of Francia, gave rise to a demand for commodities (Steuer 1990). The emporia, as the great wealth of archaeological evidence increasingly demonstrates, were rational solutions for articulating the relations between the core Christian communities with those on the peripheries, and indeed, those non-Christian communities beyond (in the remarkable case of Ribe and the later example of Haithabu situated on the Danish frontier with the Carolingians). Each centre was fashioned to serve the needs of local political forces. We should overlook neither the size of these places nor the enormous ambition encapsulated in their construction. These were dreams brought to life in designated non-places. In all likelihood, though the written sources tell us nothing of this fact, these places enshrined ideals that shaped a dialectic between the secular and ecclesistical elite on the one hand, and between the old Roman heartlands and the non-Roman periphery on the other. For the historian, then, the emporia represent a significant step in the making of the Middle Ages and a critical phase in the process of urbanisation.

4

Charlemagne as model town-maker

Where I disagree with both camps, pro- and anti-Pirenne, is that I hold that the majority of economic activity in antiquity and the early Middle Ages happened without money and without markets, that trade only played a minor role in the totality of economic activity, and that towns were not the product of trade or markets nor were they greatly dependent on them. (Samson 1994: 111)

Crucible of change

Richard Sullivan takes a an unequivocal position on the impact of Charlemagne. The great Carolingian king, he believes, is essentially a figment of European hero-worship. His achievements have been exaggerated. 'Most Carolingianists were members of an intelligentsia desperately seeking common denominators in European experience that would provide a rallying point against forces of natural and ethnic hatred, global warfare, totalitarianism, and class conflict that seemed to push Western civilization toward the fate predicted in the Spenglerian prophecy. Where better to find Europe's most precious commonalities than at the fountainhead of the European experience where presided one of Europe's few shared heroes – Karl der Grosse, Charlemagne, Carlo Magno, Charles the Great' (Sullivan 1989: 272). Sullivan, for sure, would have no wish to ascribe the birth of towns to

Charlemagne's imperial action. Charlemagne, in his terms, was a product of his age, not someone who fashioned destiny.

Chris Wickham disagrees. He has described the ninth century as the 'period of the most ambitious public power on the European continent in the whole Middle Ages up to the late thirteenth century, with elaborate and even sincere political programmes, and a legitimising rhetoric based on the king's special relationship with the poor free which fuelled its sternest critiques of aristocratic behaviour; it was also, however, the period where those same aristocrats, strengthened by their irreplaceable position at the heart of government, established a hegemony over their poor neighbours – often by force – that by no means all of them could have claimed in the two preceding centuries. It was 800, not 1000, that was in most parts of Carolingian Europe the turning-point for the establishment of local aristocratic dominance' (Wickham 1997: 198). Susan Reynolds has cogently elaborated the bases of this social revolution in Charlemagne's time: 'it is certainly possible to connect the rise of the Carolingians with new bonds of loyalty in so far as Charles Martel and his successors clearly achieved unprecedented success in marshalling their subjects to fight for them and run their government. But it is not clear that the relation between the king and either his counts or those who were now called his vassi was new in the sense that it drew on new ideas or values. What was new was the ambition and success that made it work. Once the Carolingian kingdom was established relations must have changed through the multiplication of vassi and their duties, but that was more a result of events than of new ideas. The Carolingians at their height took dues and services from all property and exercised authority over all property-holders' (Reynolds 1994: 113).

Reynolds' and Wickham's view finds a resonance in the archaeological record. Beginning with the construction of a great new palace at Paderborn in 777, the Carolingian king

4. Charlemagne as model town-maker

established a new material standard for elite dwelling
(Stiegemann and Wemhoff 1999). Taking the classical
triclinium as a model (cf. Ellis 1993), first the Carolingians,
then their aristocracy built new palaces. Studies of Aachen,
Frankfurt, Ingelheim, Naranço, Paderborn, Quiercy, Salerno,
Samoussy, Quiercy, and Zurich show just how ambitious this
new architecture was (Hodges 1993: 189). Not surprisingly, the
Anglo-Saxon kings followed suit (Hodges 1989: 129-33). These
were places that embodied the new social ethos described by
Reynolds and Wickham. Places, too, which took account of the
administration engendered by the process of regionalisation
and devolved government (Riché 1978: 41-6). The same process
was also occurring in the ecclesiastical sector of Carolingian
society. Authority was devolved to the great bishoprics and
monasteries (Devroey 1993; Toubert 1983). These places not
only built enlarged palaces for their bishops and abbots (Hodges
1993: 189), but also dedicated workshops for generating production and distribution (Sennhauser 1996). A renaissance
ideology was embodied in these new centres. The ideology was
manifest in the material and visual culture of the imperial
palaces of Paderborn, Aachen and Ingelheim, as excavations
have shown. Not surprisingly it was equally manifest in the
monasteries of the age, as excavations of places as far apart as
St Denys near Paris, Müstair in Switzerland and San Vincenzo
al Volturno have shown.

The ideology has been described by many historians as a
combination of neoclassicism with indigenous Germanic and
imported Byzantine ideas. Essential to it was a belief in rationalism. Bishop Agobard [of Lyons] complained, 'almost
everyone, nobles and commoners, city dwellers and rustics, the
aged and youth, think that hail and thunder can be caused by
human volition' (Geary 1991: 180). A scientific way of thinking
underscored the new age (Stock 1990: 130) with a new
emphasis on the writer and reader as opposed to the speaker

and hearer (1990: 102) and a concomitant intention of creating semantic maps for the exploration of new territory (1990: 108) and constructing collective memories (Geary 1994: 15). Historians are not unnaturally unsympathetic to such notions because these are difficult to assess. Yet Charlemagne propagated the virtues of reading and writing (Godman 1985: 249), and the buildings of his new age prominently displayed literacy (Hodges 1997). And while the geography of this age may have been limited by a lack of correlation with real geographical space (Lozovsky 1996: 42), nonetheless at the Carolingian court there was a keen awareness of concepts and their deployment as the significant revolution in time-keeping in Charlemagne's age illustrates. For apart from the famous elephant, Charlemagne also received an elaborate clock from the Abbasid caliph, Harun al-Rashid. This clock was 'made of brass, a marvellous mechanical contraption, in which the course of the twelve hours moved according to a water clock, with as many brazen little balls, which fell down on the hour and through their fall made a cymbal ring underneath. On this clock there were also twelve horsemen who at the end of each hour steeped out of twelve windows, closing the previously open windows by their movements' (Duncan 1998: 128-9). For Charlemagne, such timepieces represented learning and progress, much like a Model T Ford or an early Remington typewriter once signalled modernity in small isolated towns across America. But al-Rashid's gift also must have underscored the European's backwardness. Latin Christendom produced nothing approaching such a wondrous device as the caliph's clock, a situation Charlemagne reportedly understood and deplored (Duncan 1998: 129). It is hardly surprising, then, that the monasteries propagating the new ideology boasted cast bells intended to help the community regulate the services and respect time. Bells marked the major points of the reform Benedictine liturgy. The technology of making heavy bells from moulds cast in special deep pits was probably imported from the East along with the clock and elephant. To date the remains of bell-moulds (and bell-pits) found at Vreden in Germany and San Vincenzo al Volturno in Central Italy indicate that keeping time, along with the implicit knowledge involved in the production, inextricably formed part of the progressive nature of Carolingian monasteries (Drescher 1999).

Put another way, it is now commonplace to recognise that with the shift from plundering resources to investment in the agricultural economy of their estates, the Carolingian elite consciously transformed their society (Reuter 1985). Investment in estates as well as individual villages, spectacularly demonstrated by the extensive excavations of the marginal Dutch village of Kootwijk (Heidinga 1987), increased incrementally in this age (Devroey 1993). Situated on the Veluwe, perhaps thanks to presence of iron ore, the village took a planned form with the process of demolition and building inherent in creating one nucleated settlement around a grid of streets. At the same time, as we have seen, there was a marked investment in monastic workshop production (Sennhauser 1996). Output from pottery-making villages also increased significantly. Huge volumes of mass-produced tablewares and transport amphorae were made at centres in the Vorgebirge Hills close to Bonn and Cologne and distributed widely northwards into the Low Countries as well as to new centres in Westphalia. Likewise production at pottery centres in northern France in the environs of Quentovic and Rouen, as well as at ecclesistical centres such as Beauvais, were equally prodigious. Indeed, pottery production further afield in southern France, northern and central Italy, as well as in eastern England, in the case of Ipswich ware, clearly increased in scale in this era. Added to this, in 793/4 Charlemagne reformed his coinage in a bold and explicit bid to propagate the use of currency. The reform was adopted as far south as Campania, and imitated not only in England but also in Denmark (Grierson and Blackburn 1986). The use of coin, though, varied regionally. Single coin-finds are strangely uncommon in Italy and much of southern France. By contrast, large numbers of solitary finds have been made in Aquitaine and are relatively frequent in the Rhine-Seine region.

The harmonisation of the silver currency was surely the context for the inception of new regional markets – centres where the concepts of the age were represented as well as mani-fested in the form of currency exchange. Pirenne, of course, long ago made these connections. However, he believed that the new towns grew up as *suburbia* beside many old clerical *civitates* and at the foot of new fortifications *(castra)*. These fortifications had been built, so Pirenne contended, during the ninth century against the Viking invasions along the coasts and rivers of present-day Belgium and northern France. Pirenne created a duality – *suburbium/civitas* or *suburbium/castrum* – which he designated as an essential feature of the medieval town and its origins for purely military as opposed to economic reasons. In Pirenne's model it was only in the tenth century, with the revival of trade between Scandinavia and the Mediterranean, that these places acquired a mercantile purpose (Verhulst 1986a; 1986b; 1989: 4-5; 1994). It is not difficult to understand Pirenne's reading of the sources in this way, scarred as he was by his own experience of European history (see Chapter 1). The Vikings in his model were the critical factors in this history: 'the others' who first as pagans and then Christians served as a kind of *deus ex machina.*

In a characteristically lively critique of this model the American medievalist Norman Cantor addresses its flaws. 'Archaeology has not been kind to Pirenne: it tends to show remarkable continuity of urban enclaves from Roman or early post-Roman times. Just possibly the archaeologists are mistaken in the way they read their fragmentary data. As for

4. Charlemagne as model town-maker

Pirenne's insistence that the birth of cities was inspired by international trade, this was a weak point from the start. It is obvious that strictly regional trade was often the crucial factor and that towns, especially in southern England and in Germany east of the Rhine Valley, emerged as artisan and local marketing enclaves to suit the needs of the lord and his family and warriors or of the bishop and his clergy and retainers' (Cantor 1991: 129).

Obvious? Not to the Belgian historian, Adriaan Verhulst. In an enterprising reassessment of Pirenne's model, Verhulst has examined the early medieval Latin terminology related to non-rural settlements in the written texts, notably those places where tolls are generally said to have been collected: *civitates*, *castella*, and *portus*. Only the word *portus*, signifying river-port, has a commercial connotation, and, as it happens, 'the use of the word spread … during the ninth century over the whole of north-western Europe' (Verhulst 1989: 12). After surveying the extant evidence for these places in the Low Countries, Verhulst argues for the following:

(i) There was continuity of urban centres from Roman to Merovingian times.
(ii) The Merovingian urban settlements served as central places for ecclesiastical and lay administration.
(iii) During the later eighth and ninth centuries there were enlargements or new settlements of purely commercial character dominated by long-distance trade.
(iv) During the tenth century these places prospered in response to the market provided by the population of new fortifications.

Verhulst's thesis, however, published a decade ago, has been overtaken by the archaeological evidence. Huy in the Meuse valley, a signifcant *portus* in the ninth century (Verhulst 1989:

17; 1994), was evidently a major centre for ceramic production at this time, serving many parts of the Low Countries as well as eastern England (Giertz 1996). In other words, it developed as a production-distribution centre as opposed to an entrepot for long-distance trade. Further afield, Halsall has argued the same for Metz where urban renewal appears to have begun about 800 in areas outside the fortifications which had lain derelict since the fourth century (1995: 276). Cologne, not surprisingly, begins to regain its regional status as a centre in this period, closely linked to the massive ceramic production in the nearby Vorgebirge Hills (Schütte 1995; Gechter and Schütte 1998). Likewise Galinié has illustrated the same process at Tours (1988). It would be an exaggeration, on the evidence so far available, to pinpoint the rebirth of townlife to the age of Charlemagne, but with time new excavations in the Low Countries, northern France and western Germany are likely to add to the slight picture of renewed urban activity from *c.* 800.

In sum, a tenuous case may be made for the new towns of the Carolingian era being founded as ports or industrial suburbs beyond the walls of the new, enlarged palaces of the elite (Brühl 1988). With the new public order, described by Reynolds and Wickham above, these places usurped the long-held monopoly of the emporia as centres for regional production as well as toll-collecting points for long-distance trade. Unlike the 'non-places', these new towns with their histories of discontinuities paradoxically bred a sense of continuity, of history and memory (Augé 1998: 58-9). Of course, the archaeological evidence is slim as yet. Yet the logic is increasingly tenable. Just as monasteries such as St Denys, Müstair and San Vincenzo al Volturno around 790-800 created rows of workshops, with a collective interdependence and palpable use of imported technologies for mass-production purposes, so we must envisage the same around the secular centres of the age. This would largely explain the otherwise curious decline of the North Sea emporia

4. *Charlemagne as model town-maker*

– Quentovic, Dorestad, Hamwic, Lundenwic, Ipswich, Eoforwic, etc. – after *c.* 825 (Hodges and Whitehouse 1996; Metcalf and Northover 1989). The non-places, it might be said, were victims of the new rationalism, manifested as a new economic determinism.

To what are we to attribute this new economic determinism? Like the ideology itself, we may surmise, it was an amalgam of ancient, Germanic and eastern ideas. The location of the new towns had ancient roots; the social context was undeniably Germanic, as Reynolds and Wickham, cited above, have illustrated; the model towns and technologies already existed in the Abbasid caliphate. It is the latter which we find hard to accept. Nevertheless, just as Charlemagne was able to comprehend the use of an Arab clock, we must imagine that he was familiar, from the reports of pilgrims and travellers, with Arab townlife (McCormick 1998). As I noted in Chapter 2, new towns such as 'Anjar, the Umayyad city just south of Baalbek in Lebanon, as well as established centres like Aleppo, Damascus and Jerusalem, sustained the ethos of classical urbanism with roadways and pavements invaded by shops, creating the narrow alley-ways of the medieval and modern suqs (Ward-Perkins 1996: 148-52). It is difficult to imagine that these places did not have an influence. Arab silver was a fundamental resource in this period (Hodges and Whitehouse 1996). Arab silks and exotica were widely known in Italian elite circles, especially during the papacies of Hadrian I and Leo III in the late eighth and early ninth centuries (Delogu 1998b). Of course, no unequivocal evidence exists joining the urban rebirth of northwest Europe to the flourishing townlife of the Levant. Nor is any evidence likely to be found. This is a hypothesis based upon the growing body of urban archaeological evidence, its resonant echo in new analyses of the written and material sources, and a keen sense, as Pirenne put it, that 'the work of the scholar is inevitably provisional' (1912: 57-8).

Dorestad and Tiel

By way of illustration, let us consider the evidence of urban process in the ninth century at an axial point in north-western Europe – the mouth of the Rhine.

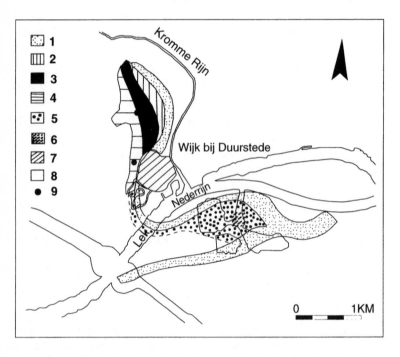

Fig. 7. Dorestad *c.* 800: 1. Partly hypothetical reconstruction of the courses of the Rhine and Lek in the Dorestad period; 2. The north harbour; 3. The north vicus; 4. The agrarian zone of the north harbour district and the central part of Dorestad; 5. The south harbour of Dorestad (hypothetical); 6. The possible location of the Roman castellum; 7. The medieval centre of Wijk bij Duurstede; 8. The present courses of the Rhine and Lek; 9. The cemetery of Dorestad (after van Es 1990).

4. Charlemagne as model town-maker

The French historian Georges Duby once dismissively enquired about Dorestad, the great emporium located at the confluence of the rivers Lek and Rhine (1974: 106): 'What was Duresteede? Archaeological investigation has revealed it as a narrow street, one kilometre in length: a road lined with warehouses wherein a few traders, for whom a parish church had been erected, lived as permanent residents.' This was a misjudged remark, nonetheless replicated twenty years later by Samson, who makes the mistake of believing the site was no more than 'one might expect at a large urban extramural monastery' (Samson 1994: 121). Van Es' majestic accounts of his excavations at Dorestad (see van Es 1990 and references therein) show beyond doubt that Dorestad was one of the great places of early medieval Europe.

Van Es traces Dorestad's history and development, demonstrating its international and regional significance. Founded around 675, it flourished until its peak in 775-825 (based on dendrochronological and numismatic evidence). A notable discovery in the excavations was the use of wooden jetties to reach the riverside as it eased away over time. The stages of the jetties are used by van Es to define the phasing of the site. In sum, the jetties were arranged in parcels – probably as properties about 20 metres wide. Behind them stood houses with their longitudinal axes towards the river. They were rectangular wooden buildings that did not differ much from the agrarian farm buildings in the nucleus of Dorestad set back from the jetties (van Es 1990: 157). Paths separated many of these buildings. 'Despite any possible deviations from the regular pattern, the *vicus* and the harbour together show a systematic layout which makes it likely that there must have been a certain measure of central and regulating authority behind it' (van Es 1990: 157). Set back from this riverside configuration was the body of the settlement (1990: 158). Only a small part of this was excavated, including a nucleus of farms and cemeteries linked by sections of trackway. Many of the farms are large wooden houses, some boat-shaped, lying in enclosed rectangular plots. Some farms had granaries as outbuildings. Most yards had one or more wells.

Verhulst and De Bock-Doehaerd have made the case that Dorestad was purely a commercial centre without any other central function (1981: 204; 207; van Es 1990: 179). Van Es questions this, but magisterially documents its status as a toll station as well as its long-distance connections down the rivers Rhine and Meuse and northwards via Medemblik (Besteman 1990) towards Denmark. He also illustrates its regional signifi- cance in the heartland of Frisia. Nevertheless, its commercial viability dissolved after *c.* 825/830. Local coinage was no longer minted after this time and the jetties fell into disrepair. A Viking attack in 834 is often thought to mark the beginning of the end, but as we have seen, the case for economic change, especially if trade was now rigorously associated with political administration, is nowhere stronger than here. Of course, the site was not wholly abandoned. At least part of it was still in use in 875, and part of the harbour may have been re-used in the tenth century (van Es 1990: 163).

Substitutes for Dorestad, following its decline, have been identified at Deventer on the river Ijssel and Tiel on the river Waal. Tiel is now the better documented, thanks to Herbert Sarfatij's investigations (1999). The town boomed in the tenth century and earned the questionable honour of enduring the last Viking raids in the region in 1006-7. In Carolingian times a plain rectangular hall-church was constructed here on an older burial ground (Sarfatij 1999: 268). By the end of the ninth century the regional nobility had founded its own monastery in Tiel dedicated to St Walburgis. So far the location of the monastery has evaded archaeological research, but Sarfatij hypothesises that the medieval town grew up alongside the river between the monastery to the west and a royal stronghold with customs responsibilities to the east. Recent excavations in what is known as the Central Quarter revealed that occupation started at the end of the ninth century with the laying out of plots at right-angles to the waterfront. Detached dwellings, narrower than the plots themselves (as at Dorestad) were erected on the wide plots. The dwellings were hall-shaped, light timber buildings of ash or beech. The occurrence of a central hearth might indicate that they functioned as dwelling houses and/or workshops in this first phase. Later the buildings were enlarged. Rubbish pits and wells were constructed in the open spaces beside the houses. The river bank was modified at the same time when a wooden quay on piles was constructed to make shallow, individual platforms which facilitated mooring (Sarfatij 1999: 271-2).

Tiel may have been an administrative centre, in the sense defined by Verhulst, but it nonetheless continued to engage in the long-distance trade with the Rhineland that had been the hallmark of Dorestad in its heyday. Pottery from the late ninth-century levels includes 65% from the Rhineland and 15% from the Meuse. Badorf relief-band amphorae and Duisberg table-wares were the pre-eminent imports. Such similarities between Tiel and its predecessor, as Sarfatij notes (1999: 274), are outweighed by the differences. The buildings themselves are an evident point of distinction. Dorestad's dwellings appear to have come largely from an agrarian background. In Tiel, on the other hand, a clear distinction seems to have developed. The dwellings so far excavated show characteristics of the large hall-like buildings with storage space associated with medieval town-housing in the region. However, Sarfatij concludes, 'what makes Tiel different and, one might say, even special in this comparison is mainly its development at a later stage. The specific layout of the harbour and the construction of large warehouses, both of which date from the second development phase (*c.* 965-1100), seem to indicate the establishment of a trading quarter of a style that differs from earlier Dorestad. The development of later Tiel is more in line with the general scaling-up and intensification of trade and urban life' (1999: 275). The chronicler Alpertus of Metz suggests that a form of merchant guild existed in the city by the eleventh century, showing, according to Sarfatij, a 'self-awareness' in developing the town's mercantile activities.

A similar comparison might be made for Rouen where the new planned town was laid out within the old Roman walls (Gauthiez 1989; Gauthiez 1993) or Quentovic and Montreuil-sur-Mer (Lebecq 1993: 81), where the former was deserted in favour of the hilltop town, or indeed, further north in western Denmark at Ribe, where the old early eighth-century emporium was relocated (Bencard, Jørgenson and Madsen 1990). The pattern was repeated in England where during the ninth century Hamwic was deserted in favour of Southampton (Andrews 1997: 255-6); Lundenwic was abandoned for Lundenburg; and Eoforwic was abandoned in favour of Jorvik. Even smaller ports such as ninth-century Norwich were relocated in the new age: in this case from the ditched enclosure north of the river Wensum to the apparently more attractive setting on the opposing bank (Ayers 1994). There were exceptions, though. Ipswich remained after the ninth century where it had always been, as did the small trading town at Medemblik, first founded in the eighth century as an outport for Dorestad on the Almere trade route to Denmark (Besteman 1990).

Defence, changes in boat technology, shifting riverbeds, and so on, have been offered as explanations. However, as the buildings of Tiel illustrate, when compared with those of Dorestad, the ninth century witnessed the emergence of a dedicated purpose driving economic development. History and memory, tied to greater devolved power, underscored investment in quays, gridded roads and sustained commercial activity.

4. Charlemagne as model town-maker

Charlemagne's impact on England

The coinage was one of the first arms of government to attract the attention of Alfred. Within the first ten years of his reign he had undertaken two major recoinages and monetary reforms and had started expanding the networks of mints. (Blackburn 1999: 122)

According to J.L. Nelson, King Alfred, England's best-known leader of the ninth century, was deeply influenced by Charlemagne: 'amid changing times, he could adapt policy to fortune; he was, in Machiavelli's sense, a virtuous prince' (Nelson 1986: 68). In many ways the clearest illustrations of Charlemagne's ideas are to be witnessed, albeit in an insular adaptation, in southern England (Hodges 1989: 152-3).

There is no real debate amongst archaeologists and historians of Anglo-Saxon England about the physical shift from emporia to market towns. At the beginning of the ninth century western Europe had monopolistic market-places – the emporia that we have seen in the previous chapter. By the end of the century, a network of new markets had been created. Martin Biddle persuasively argued that as early as 880, soon after King Alfred had reached an accord with the Danes, there were ten towns flourishing in Wessex (Biddle 1976: 137; Clark 1998: 368-73). Only the manner of the shift invokes debate. Once again the *deus ex machina* is the Vikings.

Let us consider the economic context of the new model towns before examining one, London, in a little detail. For some time historians and numismatists have resisted the argument that ninth-century England adopted currency on a significant scale, following closely the policy implemented by Charlemagne. Now, thanks to a huge number of single coin-finds made by metal-detector enthusiasts, as well as few from stratified excavations, the body of data is undeniably impressive. Michael Metcalf,

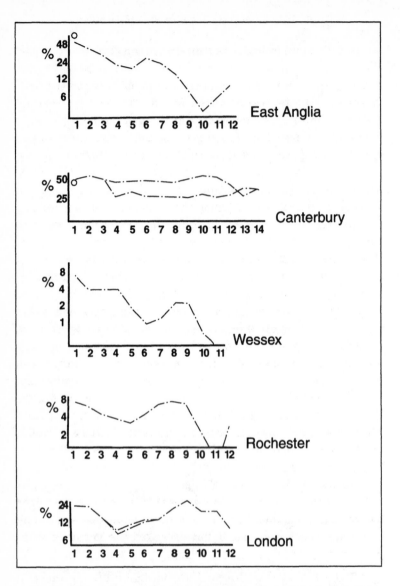

Fig. 8. Regression profiles for coins from Anglo-Saxon mints in ninth-century England; horizontal axis illustrates 25 km concentric bands from the mint (after Metcalf 1999).

building on a lifetime of studies in this field, has analysed these data to show the varying patterns of currency use in Anglo-Saxon England. His results illuminate any debate about the rebirth of towns, as well as the eclipse of the emporia with their North Sea axes by regionally-oriented market towns.

Metcalf has mapped all the single finds of ninth-century coins from England south of a line from the Mersey to the Humber (1999). His database for this study covers a 'long' ninth century, from the death of King Offa in 796 until between 899 and *c.* 910, depending on the coin series. Coins from hoards are not knowingly included. North of the Humber, he notes, few pennies from southern mints have been found. The few that occur are virtually all concentrated in York, site of the emporium of Eoforwic and its successor-town, Jorvik. The pattern which emerges is of a plentiful scatter almost everywhere in southern and eastern England, but very little from the Severn Basin and west Midlands, and almost nothing from the Welsh Marches and Wales itself. In the course of this analysis, Metcalf plots the coins against distance from the mint that produced them, and overlays the political frontiers of the period. The main points of his analysis are as follows:

(i) Carolingian coins (from Continental mints) are surprisingly numerous. These tend to be concentrated in Wessex and in the Danelaw (the eastern half of England ceded to the Danes in 878). Metcalf speculates that these were imported during what he calls 'windows of opportunity', when political control over the currency had been weakened. He hazards an estimate that these coins amounted to an output of about 4% of the dies used in England (1999: 177); much of this foreign import, he believes, was promptly recoined on entering England via Canterbury or London.

(ii) Northumbrian stycas, the debased, often bronze issues minted until the late ninth century, are found in significant numbers in the southern and eastern kingdoms of England. In his analysis of their patterning, Metcalf identifies a concentration in south Yorkshire and north Lincolnshire – the Humber region, and at the Kentish sites of Reculver, Richborough and Sandwich, close to the Wantsum Channel. Seaborne directional trade may have created these two notable ex-regional concentrations outside the Northumbrian heartland.

(iii) Looking at the overall pattern of single coin-finds, Metcalf interprets the maps to show finds thinning out to some extent towards the west and north-west. 'We may construe it in terms of a greater monetization of the economy in the east. Set against the political frontiers of the time, this means that there was a contrast between Kent and East Anglia on the one hand, and Mercia on the other, Mercia being significantly less monetized – with whatever social and political consequences that may have had' (1999: 180). This encourages Metcalf to examine movements of coins between one kingdom and another. He concludes that coins of all mints circulated widely. For example, only a third of the finds from Mercia are Mercian, and only a third of the finds from East Anglia are East Anglian. The evidence, he contends, does not sustain the use of coinage for restricted, elite purposes, but implies millions of coins crossing political boundaries and rapidly becoming mingled. Metcalf pursues this point assiduously, tracking the outputs of the principal mints and using regression analysis to see if their numbers fall off over distance in a logarithmic form. The main result of this analysis is two contrasting types of mint-profile. Canterbury, London and Rochester, which together account for sixty-six per cent of the coin finds, appear to be involved with long-distance trade. Their coins are found spread throughout southern, central and eastern England. The mints of East Anglia and in particular Wessex stand apart from this picture. Their coins are found in the Thames basin and in the Midlands, but with a predictable fall-off from source (Metcalf 1999: 195). Metcalf tacitly assumes that the former pattern may have been connected to the import of Carolingian trade via the Thames estuary and the Wantsum channel. In other words, he lays emphasis upon the extended influence of the Canterbury, London and Rochester mints being related to the import of foreign coin and other goods. In his mind, no doubt, is a picture of the Channel as an enduring flow of trade goods from the ports in the Low Countries and at the mouth of the Rhine. In practice, the archaeological pattern of international activity at London is essentially similar to those of Hamwic (in Wessex) and Ipswich (in East Anglia). An alternative explanation of these indisputably contrasting patterns may be that the Canterbury/Rochester and London thoroughfare remained opened for bullion exchange even when long-distance trade across the English Channel and North Sea was in sharp recession (Metcalf and Northover 1989). This might explain the eagerness of the West Saxon kings to control Canterbury and London at different stages of the ninth century.

Metcalf's comprehensive analysis, taken together with the incipient distribution patterns of regional and sub-regional pottery production (Hodges 1981; 1982; 1989), the distribution patterns of silver (Trewhiddle style) strap-ends (Hodges 1989: 136) and sculpture, reveals a society adopting a monetarised standard, albeit at differential rates depending on proximity to Carolingian influence. This standard, it now seems clear, was the underlying motor of the transformation of English society, making possible the transition from markets in monopolised circumstances to those serving all levels of society. How else are we to explain the extraordinary decision to abandon Anglo-

Saxon England's largest town, Lundenwic, and, over time, transfer its activities to a new planned nucleus?

A new model town

'And what of the cities and towns to be rebuilt and of others to be constructed where previously there were none?' Asser, Alfred's biographer, muses fleetingly. Perhaps the most significant new town created in the ninth century was London, or Lvndonia (as a coin of King Alfred of 886 called it), or Lundenburg, as it is called in the Anglo-Saxon Chronicle (Vince 1990). A wall-painting in London's Royal Exchange, painted in 1912, depicts King Alfred on a piebald horse amidst the ruins of the Roman city sagely approving an architect's plans for the new capital. In *People in History* (1955) R.J. Unstead takes this one step further, showing the West Saxon king directing the excavation of a new city ditch. The source of these images is a short entry in the *Anglo-Saxon Chronicle* which records that *'gesette Aelfred cyning Lundenburg'* – 'King Alfred *gesette* London-burg'. The Old English word 'gesette' has been translated as 'besieged', 'occupied', 'settled' and even 'founded', according to John Clark (1999: 36). Further adding to this interpretive confusion, Alfred's biographer Asser records that 'after the burning of cities and the massacres of people' Alfred 'restored the city of London splendidly and made it habitable again'. Needless to say, with so little to go on, precisely how, when and why London was created has constituted an enduring debate between archaeologists and historians.

Some light has been shed on this debate, first by Dyson's analysis of the written sources, and secondly by a sustained campaign of archaeological excavations. In 1978 Dyson clarified aspects of King Alfred's intentions at London. In a reassessment of two land grants for Queenhithe, an area on the shore within the Roman, medieval and modern city of

112

4. *Charlemagne as model town-maker*

London, Dyson showed that a meeting held at Chelsea in 898
or 899 between King Alfred, the Mercian ealdorman Aethelred
and Bishops Plegmund and Waerferth 'to discuss the restoration of London' when taken together with an earlier grant of
land to Bishop Waerferth, provided the context in which
streets might have been laid out around 'Aethelred's hythe',
later Queenhithe. In other words, London's new town, like its
new mint, was an initiative of Alfred's, albeit, perhaps, in
consultation with senior secular and ecclesiastical figures of
the time. It may be interesting to note that Alfred was still
apparently involved in discussions about 'the restoration of
London' – and was meeting his advisors at the royal estate of
Chelsea rather than in the new planned town. Presumably,
Alfred's plans for London were slow in being realised (Clark
1999: 38).

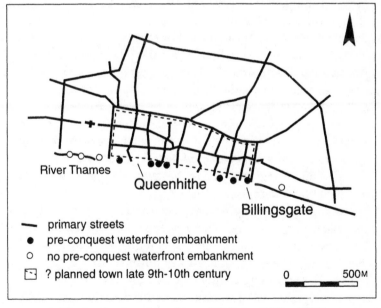

Fig. 9. A map of London *c.* 900 (after Milne 1990).

Excavations over the past twenty years, however, have illumi-
nated this brief construction history. Traces of foreshore buildings
of later ninth-century date have been discovered on the site of Bull
Wharf (now Thames Court) close to Queenhithe. Satisfactorily,
three rare half-pennies issued by Alfred's London mint supported
this dating. Elsewhere, excavations at 'Number 1 Poultry' at the
north-eastern corner of the suspected western grid of the planned
town have revealed settlement evidence of later ninth- or early
tenth-century date (Clark 1999: 38). Here, though, the arrange-
ment of the structures does not align with the Alfredian grid
proposed by Gustav Milne (1990). Milne proposed that a block
covering 30 hectares (300 metres north-south; 1000 metres east-
west) was laid out in a rectilinear pattern mirroring, perhaps, the
broad outlines of the earlier, Middle Saxon, field system that had
existed here. The initial grid, he proposed, included up to ten
streets running northwards from the river, cut by streets running
at right angles. The approximate extent of the northern edge of
the late ninth- to early tenth-century town, lying 300 metres from
the river Thames, was well to the south of the sites of the Roman
fort at Cripplegate and the Roman amphitheatre. Since Milne
advanced this hypothesis it has emerged that not all the roads,
dated by dendrochronology, appear to belong to the same date.
Moreover, a series of timber stakes on the foreshore at New Fresh
Wharf, at first interpreted as an Alfredian measure to prevent
Viking marauders from beaching their boats, after dendrochronological analysis turned out to be supports for a wharf of a
somewhat later date (Clark 1999: 37).

London's archaeologists have been puzzled by one aspect of
the settlement history. The evidence for the emporium of
Lundenwic, the precursor of Lundenburg, showed that it had
flourished in the eighth and earlier ninth centuries, as we have
seen in the preceding chapter. At its peak the town covered an
area of between 55 and 60 hectares centred around the West End
of modern London, due west of Aldwych (Cowie with Blackmore

1999: 312). Given the calculation that at least 2,000-3,000 people occupied the 40 hectares of Hamwic (Andrews 1997: 253), the population of Lundenwic at its zenith is likely to have exceeded 5,000. As at Hamwic, the evidence of recent open-area investigations suggests this was a planned town. Excavations at the Royal Opera House, for instance, unearthed evidence of buildings separated by alleys aligned end-on to a north-south gravelled road some 3 metres wide. The road had been regularly re-metalled and timber drains ran along its sides (Blackmore, Bowsher, Cowie and Malcolm 1998: 60-1). The third chronological horizon within the emporium, dating to the late eighth to early ninth centuries, characterised by shell-tempered wares, indicates that by about AD 800 Lundenwic was in decline. Indeed, the extensive settlement appears to have been largely abandoned by the mid-ninth century when London was subjected to Viking attacks (in 842 and 851) (Cowie with Blackmore 1999: 312). The chronological gap separating the two great centres either side of the river Fleet – Lundenwic to the west and Lundenburg to the east – has been closed by the discovery of a possible defensive ditch on the northern edge of the Royal Opera House excavations dated by a small hoard of Northumbrian stycas (Blackmore, Bowsher, Cowie and Malcolm 1998: 63). Interestingly, three similar hoards of this period are known from London, including a hoard of over 250 coins found in Hare Court in the Middle Temple dating to *c.* 842 when the *Anglo-Saxon Chronicle* records a great slaughter in London. Occupation, it appears, continued in parts of Lundenwic up until the middle of the century.

Taking into account Verhulst's model, as well as the evidence from Dorestad and Tiel, the vaunting history of the re-founding of London should not overly surprise us. It was, after all, part of the larger process of socio-economic change which began in Charlemagne's age with his receipt of an Indian elephant and involved, among other things, the trade in 'black stones' to Anglo-Saxon England. The decline in the earlier ninth century of Lundenwic, a town with a population numbering many thousands, cannot any longer be seriously ascribed to the Vikings. This is vulgar history. As Metcalf and Northover have shown, from the early ninth century the North Sea monetary systems were in crisis (1989). Nevertheless, Metcalf's exhaustive study of coin finds forcefully illustrates that regional economies, far from collapsing, were in fact prospering. Of course, it would be imprudent to suppose that the Vikings did not cause disruption. It would be equally imprudent to suppose that the demise of a great sprawling emporium such as Lundenwic was followed by aboriginal economics for a generation. King Alfred may not have inspected the building works at his new town as the painting in the Royal Exchange supposes, but his London mint and the evidence for the street grid shows, as at Hamwic around AD 700 and at other West Saxon burhs around AD 900 (listed in the tenth-century survey of these places known as the burghal hidage) (Hodges 1982; 1989), that he was subscribing to a conceptual programme.

Two issues puzzle us when they should not. First, the gap between Lundenwic and Lundenburh. This must have been the moment, not of collapse, but when the small new markets of the later eighth or ninth centuries first came into their own. In other words, when sub-regional centres, sustaining the monetary circulation described by Metcalf, eclipsed the monopolistic emporia (Haslam 1987; Hodges 1989: 143-9). This moment surely coincided not with the Viking attacks, but with the effective, sustainable transformation of the economy – be it in north-west Europe or Anglo-Saxon England – as the dependence on long-distance trade was superseded by the aristocratic intention to create regional trade.

The second apparently puzzling issue is that London should have evolved so slowly. Writing of London's trade privileges in the eighth century, Susan Kelly asserts that it was 'the English fulcrum ... the centre of a network of water and land communications and a commercial magnet for communities as far apart as Worcester and Minster-in-Thanet' (Kelly 1992: 26). Indeed, under King Burgred of Mercia in the 860s, according to Mark Blackburn, it was 'the most important minting place in England' (1999: 108). Yet it was Winchester that developed swiftly as Alfred assumed the reins of government over southern England. The same seems to have been the case at Jorvik, the replacement of Eoforwic, which was rapidly developed within the old Roman fortress walls under its Danish direction (Hodges 1989: 153-5). Undoubtedly the speed of development was tied to the pool of human resources available: the architects, craftsmen, road-builders and so on. Nevertheless, what is not in doubt in London, any more than York or Winchester, is that the first properties were actively engaged in artisanal activity. The craftsmen of the new towns were surely not shell-shocked survivors of the Viking raids, but descendants of the first deregulated workmen who, since the early ninth century, had been practising their crafts in an environment articulated by silver currency. These were the people who hid their savings around the Royal Opera site and in the Middle Temple. In short, these were the *laboratores* described by King Alfred in his translation of Boethius – a new social order whose physical manifestation, it might be said, was Latin Christendom's new towns.

Conclusion

Was the Carolingian age really a discrete period? Sullivan argues that it was not: 'pre-Carolingian and Carolingian history forces one to the conclusion that continuity rather than discontinuity was the essential characteristic of a long historical continuum reaching forward from the late antiquity, a continuum in which the Carolingian age constituted a not so distinctive segment' (Sullivan 1989: 281) Charlemagne was 'un souverain antique' rather than 'Europae pater' (1989: 270). The powerful influence of Henri Pirenne, so Sullivan believes, is largely responsible for this misinterpretation of the Carolingian age. Sullivan may be right to lay the origins of this periodisation at the feet of Pirenne, but he is undoubtedly mistaken when he reduces the 'long ninth century' to a continuum of development reaching back into the eighth century. The archaeology, as I have indicated, is emphatic about the rhythms of change. The late antique town did not survive beyond the seventh century in Latin Christendom. The so-called Dark Age emporia – places like Dorestad, Eoforwic, Hamwic, Lundenwic, Quentovic, Medemblik, Haithabu and Ribe – were products of different social and economic conditions. Their age, however, was over by *c.* 800 – the high point of Charlemagne's reign. The *portus*, as Verhulst has pointed out, took shape from this moment, eclipsing the hitherto monopolistic values of the emporia and introducing regional marketing, commonly articulated by an incipient monetary system. This new economic order buffered Latin Christendom against the loss of commercial interaction with the Arabs (Hodges and Whitehouse 1996), and sustained it when those dispossessed in this transformation, Baltic Sea and Arabic venturers, reinvented themselves as raiders.

Can we really maintain that Charlemagne legislated for this new economic order, just as he gave leadership to a new cultural order? Given the adoption of his monetary system from Naples to Northumberland, it is no longer imprudent to contend that this was an over-arching ambition – one that with time was to change the landscape of western Europe, giving rise to the regional market-towns which survive to this day. Clearly, though, the transition from monopolistic towns such as Dorestad and Lundenwic to devolved market-places only began in the ninth century. It was not until the eleventh century that this transition was complete. Thus economic and cultural rhythms, proceeding at different rates, have perplexed contemporaries and historians alike.

5

Conclusion

Our real research objective is the story of the role of towns rather than simply the story of the individual towns themselves. (Carver 1993: 78)

The debate about the origins of towns – and particularly about their physical form in the ninth century – will continue to absorb the interests of archaeologists and historians until the database is sufficiently ample and incontrovertible. Marxists will argue with those who favour continuity; micro-topographers will debate with advocates of macro-economic models. But a few benchmarks are now largely beyond debate. First, the debate about continuity or discontinuity between late antiquity and the age of Charlemagne is over. Archaeologists and historians now share a measure of certitude about the discontinuity in urban life that, with the special exception of Rome, characterised Latin Christendom. Secondly, the pessimists and optimists, to use Bryan Ward-Perkins' playful description of the debaters, are too polarised. New data is leading to subtler historical interpretations, as historians such as John Haldon (1999) and Adriaan Verhulst (1989; 1994) have illustrated. Thirdly, notwithstanding Wolfram Brandes' plaintive (or pitiful) plea for 'digestible' excavation reports (1999: 57), it is high time that self-respecting historians learnt the rudiments of reading excavation plans and sections, just as their counterparts in archaeology have given due respect to philology of the written texts.

There is some consensus on issues of historical substance: No one can deny the late Roman circumstances. Most classical cities came to an end between the fourth and seventh centuries. Places such as Cologne, London, Marseilles, Paris and even Rome were either deserted or else reduced to eerie shadows of their once metropolitan grandeur. As Chris Wickham has put it, 'the macroeconomics of the Roman Empire and after begins to be relatively clear ... [but] it is ... microeconomic research which we will, in the immediate future, depend on most' (Wickham 1998: 292). It goes without saying that Pirenne's thesis concerning towns in late antiquity is of only historio-graphic interest, as Delogu has cogently illustrated (see Chapter 1).

As dark earth formed over many ruined classical townscapes during the seventh and eighth centuries, Latin Christendom became a mixture of places and non-places. The places were associated with the elite – either kings and the aristocracy or the church. The chroniclers of the period laconically identified these places in terms of the ruling ethos of the 'small face-to-face' political economies of the age, to use Ian Wood's phrase (1986: 11). Put another way, the media of the age gave these places a history linked to the secular and ecclesiastical strate-gies of the time. The non-places were those sites in the interstices of this small world where foreigners might engage in controlled exchange at periodic intervals. First, these were beach fairs or markets on saints' days. Dozens, hundreds, perhaps thousands of people would camp together and transact business in valuables that could not be obtained locally. These places, sometimes the precursors of real towns or ports, I have described as type A emporia. But they were not towns so much as gatherings, the result of the economic underdevelopment of the post-classical world. Such places remained largely unknown to the writers of the age because they were temporary and without substantive history. However, they catch our eye

5. Conclusion

because they represent the seeds of European urbanism. Dorestad probably began as a periodic market-place and only after *c.* 675 was transformed, by massive investment, into a permanent town. Medemblik, an outport for Dorestad to the north, almost certainly began as a beach site (Besteman 1990). Ipswich began as a market-place on the north shore of the river Gipping in the age of Sutton Hoo, and was only later re-established as a town with a grid of streets. Hamwic may have begun the same way as a fair close to a West Saxon royal stronghold (Morton 1992: 28). Did Venice have its roots in the same sequence: initially a beach market with temporary workshops like those excavated behind the Adriatic seafront at Pescara (Staffa 1991), and then a town of immense and, to Charlemagne, dazzling proportions and potential superseding Marseilles as the gateway into the heart of Europe (Brogiolo and Gelichi 1998: 165)?

There can be no debate about the first European towns. Rome never truly died. In the ruins of the *Foro Romano*, north European pilgrims and tourists could discover townlife squeezed between the constellation of monasteries that occupied the eternal city in post-classical times. Yet Rome was not so much a town – in the sense that it had been in the age of Augustus, with streets and public buildings and residences – as a collection of elite centres with thousands of inhabitants that necessitated a bare minimum of production and procurement services (Krautheimer 1980). However, Rome without doubt became a town again in the later eighth century as, with Carolingian political support, it entertained a new vigour, midway as it was between the centres of power in the Rhineland and east Mediterranean. Delogu has convincingly charted the investment of gold, silver and silks which, alongside the new churches, cloisters and private buildings, marked a real renaissance during the papacies of Hadrian I and Leo III (1988; 1998b). Further north, the apogee of early medieval townlife, it

121

is now quite clear, was attained by the great non-places occupying the edges of the North Sea littoral: Rouen, Quentovic,
Dorestad, Hamwic, Lundenwic, Ipswich, Eoforwic, Medemblik,
Haithabu and Ribe. These places for the most part possessed
the hallmarks of later medieval towns: customs, quays, warehouses, gridded streets regularly maintained, tenements and
industrial zones. But it is what they lacked that distinguishes
them as centres. The elite were absent. Churches were virtually
absent. These places resembled the interstices of Rome without
the constellation of monasteries. Paradoxically, the elite were
present in spirit. No one now seriously doubts that the emporia
were created by powerful leaders to channel prestige goods
exchange and to control regional production. No one should
doubt the great ambition of these places. Hamwic covered more
than forty hectares; Lundenwic covered perhaps sixty hectares.
As many as five thousand people lived in these places at their
zenith, a figure at least fifty times larger than a large village or
royal estate centre. In each the gravelled streets were regularly
repaired, just as the plank-made jetties of Dorestad were
lengthened and maintained as the river bed shifted away from
the town. Venice was possibly as ambitious a centre, replacing
Marseilles as the conduit leading from the Mediterranean into
central Europe (Loseby 1998). As yet, too few excavations have
been possible, but the glimpses of the ninth-century levels are
intriguing (Brogiolo and Gelichi 1998). Further south, at the
Adriatic Sea mouth of the river Po at Comacchio, Balzaretti
(1995) believes, was another emporium.

In complete contrast to Rome, the emporia were without
history or memory, ritual or monuments. As such these places
could not be central to Charlemagne's vision of a renascent
Christendom. As we have seen, it is farfetched to believe that
new towns sprang up within the lifetime of Charlemagne,
mirroring the now apparent transformation of small monasteries into large, nucleated centres of civilisation (Hodges

5. Conclusion

1995). The transformation of the monasteries into centres of estate production and distribution provided the motor articulating Charlemagne's vision. Regional towns such as Brescia and Verona were transformed more slowly, as were one-time centres as diverse as Marseilles (Loseby 1998), Cologne and Tours (Galinié 1988) to the north of the Alps. The regions of western Europe essentially evolved at differing rates – the Meuse region possibly before the Rhine, and the Seine following afterwards (Verhulst 1989). Certainly, towns were in fashion by the mid-ninth century in Italy when new towns were created at Rome (the so-called Leonine city), Centocelle (near Civitavecchia) in the papal kingdom and Sicopolis (near Capua) in the Kingdom of Benevento (Marazzi 1994). Each was awarded great defences worthy of ancient cities, streets and, probably, an array of elite dwellings and churches.

Beyond the reach of Carolingian power, southern England and southern Denmark responded swiftly to the ethos of the new age. Northumbria, by contrast, was slow to respond, as Metcalf has shown (1999). As a result, Hamwic and Lundenwic had to compete with emergent centres in southern England (Haslam 1987): in East Anglia Ipswich now had to compete with incipient new centres at Norwich and Thetford. Long before the turn of the millennium this new urban pattern had solidified to take the shape that would endure until industrialisation.

Did Charlemagne introduce this bold new economic strategy with its implications for the rebirth of towns? Whatever I have proposed in Chapters 1-4, the definitive answer will remain unknown. It is a matter for conjecture whether he was influenced by his experience of Italy in the 770s and, with his knowledge of Byzantium and the Caliphate, recognised the potential of reviving the towns of his empire as he invested in developing a cultural revolution. It is a matter for conjecture, too, whether the emergent merchant class, the so-called third order, who provided the workforce in the emporia, produced a new non-clerical energy on which, with strong leadership, kings such as Charlemagne, Offa and, later, Alfred, could effectively draw. Lastly, one can only speculate whether Charlemagne and his contemporaries were influenced by the pilgrims and traders who had been to Palestine and had seen the great Abbasid places of the Levant where townlife persisted uninterrupted in its Arabic reformulation of the classical concept. Any mention of such admiration was heresy. Yet, as the archaeology of the eighth and ninth centuries becomes a little more familiar, we must seriously envisage that, just as the Baltic Sea was regularly in contact with the Abbasid caliphate, so the Carolingian and Arabic worlds were far more interconnected than the writers of the age would have their readers believe.

The debate will gradually be resolved as the ninth-century levels of places such as Cologne and Tours, Lucca and Winchester are carefully exposed and recorded. This is the call to arms for microregional research (and sound stratigraphical excavations). It will be some decades yet before a picture of places such as Paris or Venice in the ninth century can be reconstructed as thoroughly as a first-century imperial city. Above all, there is a need to chart the rebirth or revival of craft technologies – such as those documented in the excavations of the workshops at San Vincenzo al Volturno in central Italy – and pinpoint the genesis of technologies which underpinned the making of the Middle Ages.

One conclusion is beyond debate: while the archaeology of the ninth-century emporia, like that of the renascent monasteries, is rich in a distinctive material culture, the old historic centres with their Roman wall circuits, soon to take new shape, possess only limited islands of occupation not unlike the type A emporia (or periodic fairs) and only come to resemble the emporia in their affluent material richness in the tenth and eleventh centuries. In short, the non-places of the eighth and ninth centuries, beyond the reach of written history, are now

5. *Conclusion*

measures of an indisputably important episode in the history of western Europe. Archaeology has contributed significantly to a paradigmatic change in our understanding of the history of medieval towns in Europe.

Bibliography

Andreolli, B. and Montanari, M. (1983) *L'Azienda Curtense in Italia*, Bologna, CLUEB.

Andrews, P. (1987) *Excavations at Hamwic*, vol. 2, York, Council for British Archaeology Research Report 109.

Arbman, H. (1937) *Schweden und das karolingische Reich*, Stockholm, Almqvist and Wiksell.

Arnold, B. (1990) The past as propaganda in Nazi Germany, *Antiquity* 64: 464-78.

Astill, G. (1985) Archaeology, economics and early medieval Europe, *Oxford Journal of Archaeology* 4: 215-31.

Attenborough, F.L. (1922) (ed.) *The Laws of the Earliest English Kings*, Cambridge, Cambridge University Press.

Augé, M. (1995) *Non-Places. Introduction to an Anthropology of Supermodernity* (trans. John Howe), London, Verso.

Augé, M. (1998) *A Sense for the Other: The Timeliness and Relevance of Anthropology* (trans. Amy Jacobs), Stanford, Stanford University Press.

Ayers, B. (1994) *Norwich*, London, Batsford.

Balzaretti, R. (1995) Cities, emporia: local economics in the Po valley, c. 700-875, in N. Christie and S. Loseby (eds) *Towns in Transition: Urban Evolution in Late Antiquity and the Early Middle Ages*, Aldershot, Scolar Press: 212-34.

Bedini, S.A. (1998) *The Pope's Elephant*, London, Carcanet.

Bencard, M., Jørgenson, L. and Madsen (1990) *Ribe Excavations 1970-1976*, vol. 4, Esbjerg, Ribe excavations.

Bertelli, C. (1987) (ed.) *Milano. Una Capitale da Ambrogio ai Carolingi*, Milan, Electa.

Besteman, J.C. (1990) The pre-urban development of Medemblik, in H.A. Heidinga and H.H. van Regeteren Altena (eds) *Medemblik and Monnichendam: Aspects of Medieval Urbanization in Northern Holland*, Assen, Van Gorcum: 1-30.

Bibliography

Biddle, M. (1976) The Towns, in D.M. Wilson (ed.) *The Archaeology of Anglo-Saxon England*, London, Methuen: 99-150.

Blackburn, M. (1999) The London mint in the reign of Alfred, in M. Blackburn and D. Dumville (eds) *Kings, Currency and Alliances*, Woodbridge, Boydell and Brewer: 105-23.

Blackmore, L., Bowsher, D., Cowie, R. and Malcolm, G. (1998) Royal Opera House, *Current Archaeology* 158: 60-3.

Blindheim, C., Heyerdahl-Larsen, B. and Tollnes, R. (1981) *Kaupang-funnene 1*, Oslo, Norske Oldfunn, 11.

Blindheim, C. and Heyerdahl-Larsen, B. (1995) *Kaupang-funnene 2*, Oslo, Norske Oldfunn, 16.

Bloch, M. (1954) *The Historian's Craft*, Manchester, Manchester University Press.

Bourdieu, P. (1996) Über die Beziehung zwischen Gëschichte und Soziologie in Frankreich und Deutschland, *Gëschichte und Soziologie* 22: 62-89.

Brandes, W. (1999) Byzantine cities in the seventh and eighth centuries – different sources, different histories, in G-P. Brogiolo and B. Ward-Perkins (eds) *The Idea and Ideology of the Town between Late Antiquity and the Early Middle Ages*, The Hague, E.J. Brill: 25-58.

Braudel, F. (1977) *Afterthoughts on Material Civilization and Capitalism*, Baltimore, Johns Hopkins University Press.

Brisbane, M. (1988) Hamwic (Saxon Southampton): an eighth-century port and production centre, in R. Hodges and B. Hobley (eds) *The Rebirth of Towns in the West AD 700-1050*, London, Council for British Archaeology Research Report 68: 101-8.

Brogiolo, G.P. and Gelichi, S. (1998) *La Città nell'Alto Medioevo Italiano*, Rome, Laterza.

Brogiolo, G.P. and Ward-Perkins, B. (1999) (eds) *The Idea and Ideology of the Town between Late Antiquity and the Early Middle Ages*, The Hague, E.J. Brill.

Brown, P. (1967) *Augustine of Hippo*, London, Faber and Faber.

Brühl, C. (1988) Problems of continuity of Roman *civitates* in Gaul, as illustrated by the interrelation of cathedral and *palatium*, in R. Hodges and B. Hobley (eds) *The Rebirth of Towns in the West AD 700-1050*, London, Council for British Archaeology Research Report 68: 43-6.

Cantor, N.F. (1991) *Inventing the Middle Ages*, New York, Morrow.

Carver, M.O.H. (1993) *Arguments in Stone: Archaeological Research and the European Town in the First Millennium*, Oxford, Oxbow Books.

Ceci, M. (1992) Note sulla circolazione delle lucerne a Roma nell' VIII secolo: i contesti della Crypta Balbi, *Archeologia Medievale* 19: 749-64.

Christie, N. and Loseby, S. 1995 (eds) *Towns in Transition: Urban Evolution in Late Antiquity and the Early Middle Ages*, Aldershot, Scolar Press.

Clark, H.B. (1998) Proto-towns and towns in Ireland and Britain in the ninth and tenth centuries, in H.B. Clarke, M.N. Mhaonaigh and R. O'Floinn (eds) *Ireland and Scandinavia in the Early Viking Age*, Dublin, Four Courts Press: 331-80.

Clark, J. (1999) King Alfred's London and London's King Alfred, *London Archaeologist* 9: 35-8.

Coates-Stephens, R. (1997) Dark Age architecture in Rome, *Papers of the British School at Rome* 65: 177-232.

Coupland, S. (1990) Money and coinage under Louis the Pious, *Francia* 17: 23-48.

Cowie, R. with Blackmore, L. (1999) Excavation and mitigation in *Lundenwic*: a case study, *London Archaeologist* 8: 311-20.

Crawford, J.S. (1990) *The Byzantine Shops at Sardis*, Harvard, Harvard University Press.

Delogu, P. (1988) The rebirth of Rome in the eighth and ninth centuries, in R. Hodges and B. Hobley (eds) *The Rebirth of Towns in the West, AD 700-1050*, London, Council for British Archaeology Research Report 68: 32-42.

Delogu, P. (1998a) Reading Pirenne again, in R. Hodges and W. Bowden (eds) *The Sixth Century: Production, Distribution and Demand*, The Hague, E.J. Brill: 15-40.

Delogu, P. (1998b) L'importazione di tessuti preziosi e il sistema economico romano nel IX secolo, in P. Delogu (ed.) *Roma Medievale. Aggiornamenti*, Florence, All'Insegna del Giglio: 123-41.

Devroey, J-P. (1993) *Études sur le Grand Domaine Carolingienne*, Aldershot, Variorum.

Drescher, H. (1999) Die Glöcken der karolingerzeitlichen Stiftskirche in Vreden, Kreis Ahaus, in *Karl der Grosse und Papst Leo III in Paderborn. Kunst und Kültur der Karolingerzeit*, Mainz, von Zabern: 356-64.

Duby, G. (1974) *The Early Growth of the European Economy*, London, Weidenfeld and Nicolson.

Duby, G. (1982) *The Three Orders. Feudal Society Imagined*, London, University of Chicago Press.

Duncan, D.E. (1998) *The Calendar*, London, Fourth Estate.

Bibliography

Dutton, P.E. (1998) (ed.) *Charlemagne's Courtier: The Complete Einhard*, Peterborough (Ontario), Broadview Press.

Dyson, T. (1978) Two Saxon land grants for Queenhithe, in J. Bird, H. Chapman and J. Clark (eds) *Collectanea Londiniensia* (London Middlesex Archaeology Society Special Paper 2): 200-15.

Eldredge, N. and Gould, S.J. (1972) Punctuated equilibria: an alternative to phyletic gradualism, in T.J.M. Schopf (ed.) *Models in Paleobiology*, San Francisco: Freeman, Cooper and Co.: 82-115.

Eley, G. and Nield, K. (1993) Starting over: the present, the postmodern and the moment of social history, *Social History* 18: 219-33.

Ellis, S. (1993) Power architecture and decor: how the Late Roman aristocrat appeared to his guests, in E.K. Gazda (ed.) *Roman Art in the Private Sphere*, Ann Arbor, University of Michigan Press: 117-56.

Evans, R.J. (1997) *In Defence of History*, London, Granta Books.

Fink, C. (1989) *Marc Bloch: A Life in History*, Cambridge, Cambridge University Press.

Finley, M.I. (1981) The Ancient City, in M.I. Finley, *Economy and Society in Ancient Greece*, Harmondsworth, Penguin: 3-21.

Foss, C. (1977) Archaeology and the 'Twenty Cities' of Byzantine Asia, *American Journal of Archaeology* 81: 469-81.

Foss, C. (1979) *Ephesus after Antiquity*, Cambridge, Cambridge University Press.

Foss, C. (1997) Syria in transition, AD 550-750: an archaeological approach, *Dumbarton Oaks Papers* 51: 189-269.

Funari, P.P.A. (1999) Historical archaeology from a world perspective, in P.P.A. Funari, M. Hall and S. Jones (eds) *Historical Archaeology: Back from the Edge*, London, Routledge: 37-60.

Galinié, H. (1988) Reflections on early medieval Tours, in R. Hodges and B. Hobley (eds) *The Rebirth of Towns in the West AD 700-1050*, London, Council for British Archaeology Research Report 68: 57-62.

Gauthiez, B. (1993) La re-occupation plantifée de la Cité de Rouen au Haut Moyen Age, in J. Stratford (ed.) *Medieval Art, Architecture and Archaeology at Rouen*, London, The British Archaeological Association Conference Transactions for the year 1986: 12-19.

Gauthiez, N. (1989) Rouen pendant le Haut Moyen Age, in H. Atsma (ed.) *La Neustrie: les Pays au Nord de la Loire de 650 à 850*, Sigmaringen, Thorbecke: 1-20.

Geary, P. (1991) *Living with the Dead in the Middle Ages*, Ithaca, Cornell University Press.

Geary, P. (1994) *Phantoms of Remembrance. Memory and Oblivion at the End of the First Millennium*, Princeton, Princeton University Press.

Gechter, M. and Schütte, S. (1998) Zwischen St. Alban und Judenviertel in Köln, *Rheinische Heimatpflege* 35: 37-56.

Geertz, C. (1973) Thick description: toward an interpretive theory of culture, in C. Geertz, *The Interpretation of Cultures*, New York, Basic Books: 3-30.

Giddens, A. (1971) *Capitalism and Modern Social Theory*, Cambridge, Cambridge University Press.

Giertz, W. (1996) Middle Meuse Valley ceramics of Huy-type: a preliminary analysis, *Medieval Ceramics* 20: 33-61.

Godman, P. (1985) *Poetry of the Carolingian Renaissance*, London, Duckworth.

Gomez Becerra, A. (1995) El problamiento altomedieval en la coasta de Granada, *Studia Historica. Historia Medieval* 13: 59-92.

Greenhalgh, M. (1989) *The Survival of Roman Antiquities in the Middle Ages*, London, Duckworth.

Grierson, P. and Blackburn, M. (1986) *Medieval European Coinage*, vol. 1: *The Early Middle Ages (fifth-tenth centuries)* Cambridge, Cambridge University Press.

Gutiérrez Lloret, S. (1998) Eastern Spain in the sixth century in the light of archaeology, in R. Hodges and W. Bowden (eds) *The Sixth Century: Production, Distribution and Consumption*, The Hague, E.J. Brill: 161-84.

Haldon, J. (1990) *Byzantium in the Seventh Century: The Transformation of a Culture*, Cambridge, Cambridge University Press.

Haldon, J. (1999) The Idea of the Town in the Byzantine Empire, in G.P. Brogiolo and B. Ward-Perkins (eds) *The Idea and Ideology of the Town between Late Antiquity and the Early Middle Ages*, The Hague, E.J. Brill: 1-23.

Hall, R. (1984) *The Viking Dig*, London, Bodley Head.

Halsall, G. (1995) *Settlement and Social Organization: The Merovingian Region of Metz*, Cambridge, Cambridge University Press.

Harrison, R. (1986) *Excavations at Saraçhane in Istanbul I*, Princeton, Princeton University Press.

Haslam, J. (1987) Market and fortress in England in the reign of Offa, *World Archaeology* 19: 76-93.

Bibliography

Hayes, J. (1992) *Excavations at Saraçhane in Istanbul 2*, Princeton, Princeton University Press.

Heidinga, H.A. (1987) *Medieval Settlement and Economy North of the Lower Rhine. Archaeology and History of Kootwijk and the Veluwe (the Netherlands)*, Assen, Van Gorcum.

Heitz, C. (1980) *L'Architecture religieuse carolingienne*, Paris, Picard.

Hill, D. et al. (1990) Quentovic defined, *Antiquity* 64: 51-8.

Hillenbrand, R. (1999) 'Anjar and Early Islamic Urbanism, in G.P. Brogiolo and B. Ward-Perkins (eds) *The Idea and Ideology of the Town between Late Antiquity and the Early Middle Ages*, The Hague, E.J. Brill: 59-98.

Hines, J. (1994) North Sea trade and the proto-urban sequence, *Achaeologia Polona* 32: 7-26.

Hinton, D. (1996) *The Gold, Silver and Other Non-Ferrous Alloy Objects from Hamwic* (Southampton Finds vol. 2), Stroud, Alan Sutton.

Hodges, R. (1981) *The Hamwih Pottery*, London, Council for British Archaeology Research Report No. 37.

Hodges, R. (1982) *Dark Age Economics: The Origins of Towns and Trade, AD 600-1000*, London, Duckworth.

Hodges, R. (1989) *The Anglo-Saxon Achievement: Archaeology and the Beginnings of English Society*, London, Duckworth.

Hodges, R. (1993) (ed.) *San Vincenzo al Volturno 1*, London, British School at Rome.

Hodges, R. (1994) In the Shadow of Pirenne: San Vincenzo al Volturno and the revival of Mediterranean commerce, in R. Francovich and G. Noyé (eds) *La Storia dell' Alto Medioevo Italiano (VI–X secolo) alla Luce dell'Archeologia*, Florence, All'Insegna del Giglio: 109-27.

Hodges, R. (1995) (ed.) *San Vincenzo al Volturno 2*, London, British School at Rome.

Hodges, R. (1997) *Light in the Dark Ages: The Rise and Fall of San Vincenzo al Volturno*, London, Duckworth.

Hodges, R. (1999) Dark Age Economics revisited, in H. Sarfatij, W. Verwers and P. Woltering (eds) *In Discussion with the Past. Archaeological Studies presented to W.A. van Es*, Zwolle, ROB/SPA: 227-32.

Hodges, R. and Moran, M. (2000) (eds) *Twenty Years at San Vincenzo al Volturno*, Oxford, Oxbow Books.

Hodges, R. and Whitehouse, D. (1983) *Mohammed, Charlemagne and the Origins of Europe*, London, Duckworth.

Hodges, R. and Whitehouse, D. (1996) *Mahomet, Charlemagne et les origines de l'Europe*, Paris, P. Lethielleux.

Hodges, R. et al. (1997) Late-antique and Byzantine Butrint: interim report on the port and its hinterland (1994-95), *Journal of Roman Archaeology* 10: 207-34.

Holwerda, J.H. (1930) Opgravingen van Dorestad, *Oudheidkundige Mededelingen* 9: 32-93.

Hope-Taylor, B. (1977) *An Anglo-British Centre of Early Northumbria*, London, H.M.S.O.

Horn, W. and Born, E. (1979) *The Plan of St Gall*, Berkeley, University of California Press.

Hyenstrand, E. (1992) Early discoveries in the black earth, in B. Ambrosiani and H. Clarke (eds) *Early Investigations and Future Plans*, Stockholm, Birka Studies 1: 23-51.

Jankuhn, H. (1939) Haithabu and the Danewerk, *Antiquity* 13: 103-5.

Johnson, M.H. (1999) Rethinking historical archaeology, in P.P.A. Funari, M. Hall and S. Jones (eds) *Historical Archaeology: Back from the Edge*, London, Routledge: 23-66.

Kelly, S. (1992) Trading privileges from eighth-century England, *Early Medieval Europe* 1: 3-28.

Kemp, R.L. (1996) *Anglian Settlement at 46-54 Fishergate* (The Archaeology of York; Anglian York 7/1), York, Council for British Archaeology.

Kennedy, H. (1985a) The last century of Byzantine Syria: a reinterpretation, *Byzantinische Förschungen* X: 141-83.

Kennedy, H. (1985b) From *polis* to *Madina*: urban change in late antique and early Islamic Syria, *Past and Present* 106: 3-27.

Krautheimer, R. (1980) *Rome: Profile of a City, 312-1308*, Princeton, Princeton University Press.

Kuhn, T. (1962) *The Structure of Scientific Revolutions*, Chicago, Chicago University Press.

Lebecq, S. (1989) La Neustrie et la Mer, in H. Atsma (ed.) *La Neustrie: les Pays au Nord de la Loire de 650 à 850*, Sigmaringen, Thorbecke: 405-40.

Lebecq, S. (1991) Pour une histoire parallèle de Quentovic et Dorestad, in J-M. Devosquel and A. Dierkens (eds) *Villes et Campagnes au Moyen Age, Melanges Georges Despy*, Liege: 415-28.

Lebecq, S. (1993) Quentovic: un état de la question, *Studien zur Sachsenförschung* 8: 73-82.

Lebecq, S. (1994) Entre Manche et Mer du Nord, entre Grande-

Bibliography

Bretagne et Continent, les relations à travers le detroit dans les premiers siècles médievaux, in S. Curveiller (ed.) *Les Champs Relationnels en Europe du Nord et du Nord-Ouest des Origines à la Fin du Premier Empire*, Calais, Municipalité de Calais: 29-43.

Le Goff, J. (1980) *Time, Work and Culture in the Middle Ages*, Chicago, Chicago University Press.

Le Goff, J. (1988) The wilderness in the medieval west, in J. Le Goff, *The Medieval Imagination*, Chicago, Chicago University Press: 47-59.

Le Goff, J. (1990) Le travail dans les systèmes de valeur de l'occident médievale, in J. Hamesse and C. Muraille-Samaran (eds) *Le Travail au Moyen Age: Une Approche Interdisciplinaire*, Louvain: 7-22.

Le Maho, J. (1993) Le groupe épiscopal de Rouen du IVe au Xe siècle, in J. Stratford (ed.) *Medieval Art, Architecture and Archaeology at Rouen*, London, British Archaeological Association Conference Proceedings for the year 1986: 20-30.

Levi-Strauss, C. (1989) *Triste Tropiques*, London, Fontana.

Llewellyn, P. (1986) The Popes and the constitution in the eighth century, *English History Review* 101: 42-67.

Lohrmann, D. (1989) Le moulin à eau dans le cadre de l'économie rurale de la Neustrie (VIIe-IXe siècles), in H. Atsma (ed.) *La Neustrie. Les Pays au Nord de la Loire de 650 à 850*, Sigmaringen, Thorbecke: 367-404.

Loseby, S.T. (1998) Marseille and the Pirenne Thesis, I: Gregory of Tours, the Merovingian kings and 'un grand port', in R. Hodges and W. Bowden (eds) *The Sixth Century: Production, Distribution and Demand*, The Hague, E.J. Brill: 203-30.

Lozovsky, N. (1996) Carolingian geographical tradition: was it geography? *Early Medieval Europe* 5: 25-43.

Lyon, B. (1974) *Henri Pirenne: A Biographical and Intellectual Study*, Ghent, E. Story-Scientia.

Manacorda, D. and Saguì, L. (1995) L'esedra della Crypta Balbi e il monastero di S. Lorenzo in Pallacinis, *Archeologia Laziale* XXI: 121-34.

Mango, C. (1985) *Le Développement Urbain de Constantinople (VIe-VIIe siècles)*, Paris.

Mann, M. (1986) *The Sources of Social Power*, vol. 1: *A History of Power from the Beginning to 1760 AD*, Cambridge, Cambridge University Press.

Marazzi, F. (1994) Le 'città nuove' pontificie e l'insediamento laziale nel IX secolo, in R. Francovich and G. Noyé (eds) *La Storia dell' Alto Medioevo Italiano (VI-X secolo) alla Luce dell' Archeologia*, Florence, All' Insegna del Giglio: 251-78.

McCormick, M. (1998) Bateaux de vie, bateaux de mort. Maladie, commerce, transports annonaires et le passage économique du bas-empire au moyen âge, *Settimane di Studio del Centro Italiano di Studi sull'Alto Medioevo* (3-9 Aprile 1997): 35-122.

Menegnini, R. and Santangeli Valenzani, R. (1996) Episode di trasformazione del paesaggio urbano nella Roma altomedievale, *Archeologia Medievale* 23: 53-99.

Metcalf, M. (1994) The beginnings of coinage in the North Sea coastlands: a Pirenne-like hypothesis, in B. Ambrosiani and H. Clarke (eds) *The Twelfth Viking Congress. Birka Studies Volume 3*, Stockholm, Almqvist and Wiksell: 196-214.

Metcalf, D.M. (1999) The monetary economy of ninth-century England south of the Humber, in M. Blackburn and D. Dumville (eds) *Kings, Currency and Alliances*, Woodbridge, Boydell and Brewer: 167-97.

Metcalf, D.M. and Northover, J.P. (1989) Coinage alloys from the time of Offa and Charlemagne to c. 854, *Numismatic Chronicle* 149: 101-20.

Milne, G. (1990) King Alfred's plan for London, *London Archaeologist* 8: 206-7.

Morris, R. (1989) *Churches in the Landscape*, London, Dent.

Morton, A.D. (1992) (ed.) *Excavations at Hamwic*, vol. 1, York, Council for British Archaeology Research 84.

Nees, L. (1991) *A Tainted Mantle: Hercules and the Classical Tradition at the Carolingian Court*, Philadelphia, University of Pennsylvania Press.

Nelson, J.L. (1986) 'A king across the sea': Alfred in Continental perspective, *Transactions of the Royal Historical Society* 36: 45-68.

Nelson, J.L. (1988) Kingship and empire, in J.H. Burns (ed.) *The Cambridge History of Medieval Political Thought c. 350 – c. 1450*, Cambridge, Cambridge University Press: 211-51.

Nilsson, L. and Lilja, S. (1996) (eds) *The Emergence of Towns: Archaeology and Early Urbanization in Non-Roman, North-West Europe* (Studies in Urban History 14) Stockholm.

Noonan, T. (1984) The regional composition of ninth-century dirhem hoards from European Russia, *Numismatic Chronicle* 144: 153-65.

Noonan, T. (1994) The Vikings in the east: coins and commerce, in B. Ambrosiani and H. Clarke (eds) *The Twelfth Viking Congress. Birka*

Bibliography

Studies Volume 3, Stockholm, Alqvist and Wiksell: 215-36.

Oddy, W.A. (1972) Analyses of Lombard tremisses by the specific-gravity method, *Numismatic Chronicle* ser. VII, 12: 193-215.

Oddy, W.A. (1974) Analysis of the gold coinage of Beneventum, *Numismatic Chronicle* ser. VII, 14: 78-109.

Oddy, W.A. (1988) The debasement of the provincial Byzantine gold coinage from the seventh to the ninth centuries, in W. Hahn and W.E. Metcalf (eds) *Studies in Early Byzantine Gold Coinage* (Numismatic Studies, 17), New York: 135-42.

Ovitt, G. (1986) Manual labour and early medieval monasticism, *Viator* 17: 1-18.

Parsons, T. (1928) Capitalism in recent German literature: Sombart and Weber, *Journal of Political Economy* 36: 641-61.

Peacock, D.P.S. (1997) Charlemagne's black stones: the re-use of Roman columns in early medieval Europe, *Antiquity* 71: 709-15.

Pentz, P. (1992) *The Invisible Conquest: The Ontogenesis of Sixth and Seventh Century Syria*, Copenhagen, National Museum.

Pertusi, A. (1968) Ordinamenti militari, guerre in occidente e teorie dei Bizantini (secc. VI-X), *Settimane di Studio del Centro Italiano di Studi sull'Alto Medioevo* 15: 631-700.

Pirenne, H. (1895) L'origine des constitutions urbaines, *Revue Historique* LVII: 57-98.

Pirenne, H. (1912) *Manifestation en l'hônneur de M. le Professeur Henri Pirenne*, Mons.

Pirenne, H. (1925) *Medieval Cities* (trans. F.D. Halsey), Princeton, Princeton University Press.

Pirenne, H. (1939) *Mohammed and Charlemagne*, London, Unwin.

Potter, T.W. (1995) *Towns in Late Antiquity: Iol Caesarea and its Context*, Oxford, Sheffield Academic Press.

Potter, T.W. and King, A.C. (1997) *Excavations at the Mola di Monte Gelato*, London, British School at Rome.

Randsborg, K. (1991) *The First Millennium*, Cambridge, Cambridge University Press.

Renfrew, C. (1975) Trade as action at distance: questions of integration and communication, in J. Sabloff and C.C. Lamberg-Karlovsky (eds) *Ancient Civilisation and Trade*, Albuquerque, University of New Mexico Press: 3-59.

Renfrew, C. and Cherry, J.F. (1986) (eds) *Peer-Polity Inter-action and Socio-Political Change*, Cambridge, Cambridge University Press.

Reuter, T. (1985) Plunder and tribute in the Carolingian empire,

Transactions of the Royal Historical Society 35: 75-94.

Reynolds, S. (1994) *Fiefs and Vassals*, Oxford, Clarendon Press.

Ricci, M. (1997) Relazioni culturali e scambi commerciali nell'Italia centrale romano-longobarda alla luce della Crypta Balbi in Roma, in L. Paroli (ed.) *L'Italia Centro-Settentrionale in Età Longobarda*, Florence, All'Insegna del Giglio: 239-73.

Riché, P. (1978) *Daily Life in the World of Charlemagne* (trans. J. McNamara), Liverpool, Liverpool University Press.

Rovelli, A. (1998) La circolazione monetaria a Roma nei secoli VII e VII. Nuovi dati per la storia economica di Roma nell' alto medioevo, in P. Delogu (ed.) *Roma Medievale. Aggiornamenti*. Florence, All'Insegna del Giglio: 79-91.

Saguì, L. (1993) Crypta Balbi (Roma): conclusione delle indagini archeologiche nell'esedra del monumento romano. Relazione preliminare, *Archeologia Medievale* 20: 409-18.

Saguì, L. (1998a) Indagini archeologiche a Roma: nuovi dati sul VII secolo, in P. Delogu (ed.) *Roma Medievale. Aggiornamenti*. Florence, All'Insegna del Giglio: 63-73.

Saguì, L. (1998b) (ed.) *Ceramica in Italia: VI-VII secolo*, Florence, All'Insegna del Giglio.

Saguì, L., Ricci, M. and Romei, D. (1997) Nuovi dati ceramologici per la storia economica di Roma tra VII e VIII secolo, in G. Demians D'Archimbaud (ed.) *La Céramique Médievale en Mediterranée* (Actes du VIe congrès de AIECM) Aix-en-Provence, Narration Editions: 35-48.

Sahlins, M. (1974) *Stone Age Economics*, London, Tavistock Press.

Samson, R. (1994) Populous Dark-Age towns: the Finleyesque approach, *Journal of European Archaeology* 2: 97-129.

Sarfatij, H. (1999) Tiel in succession to Dorestad, in H. Sarfatij, W. Verwers and P. Woltering (eds) *In Discussion with the Past*, Zwolle, SPA/ROB: 267-78.

Scales, P.C. (1997) Cordoba under the Umayadds, in G. De Boe and F. Verhaeghe (eds) *Urbanism in Medieval Europe I*, Zellik, Proceedings of the Conference on Medieval Europe: 175-82.

Schütte, S. (1995) Continuity problems and authority structures in Cologne, in G. Ausenda (ed.) *After Empire*, Woodbridge, Boydell and Brewer: 163-75.

Sennett, R. (1994) *Flesh and Stone. The Body and the City in Western Civilization*, New York, Norton.

Sennhauser, H-R. (1996) (ed.) *Wöhn- und Wirtschaftsbauten frühmittel-*

alterlicher Klöster, Zurich, Hochschulverlag.

Smith, C.A. (1976) Exchange systems and the spatial distribution of elites: the organisation of stratification in agrarian societies, in C.A. Smith (ed.) *Regional Analysis*, vol. 2, London, Academic Press: 309-74.

Sombart, W. (1902) *Der moderne Kapitalismus*, Berlin.

Spieser, J-M. (1989) L'evolution de la ville byzantine de l'epoque paléochrêtienne a l'iconoclasme, in *Hommes et Richesses dans l'Empire byzantin I*, Paris, P. Lethielleux: 97-106.

Staffa, A. (1991) Scavi nel centro storico di Pescara, *Archeologia Medievale* 18: 201-367.

Steuer, H. (1990) Archaeology and history: proposals on the social structure of the Merovingian kingdom, in K. Randsborg (ed.) *The Birth of Europe*, Rome, Danish Institute in Rome: 100-22.

Stiegemann, C. and Wemhoff, M. (1999) (eds) *799 Kunst und Kültur der Karolingerzeit. Karl der Grosse und Päpst Leo III in Paderborn*, Mainz, Von Zabern.

Stock, B. (1990) *Listening for the Text*, Baltimore, Johns Hopkins University Press.

Sullivan, R. (1989) The Carolingian Age: reflections on its place in the history of the Middle Ages, *Speculum* LXIV: 267-306.

Toubert, P. (1983) Il sistema curtense: la produzione e lo scambio interno in Italia nel secoli VIII-X, in P. Toubert (ed.) *Economia Naturale. Economia Monetaria*, Turin, Einaudi: 5-65.

Ulriksen, J. (1994) Danish sites and settlements with a maritime context, AD 200-1200, *Antiquity* 68: 797-811.

Van Es, W.A. (1969) Excavations at Dorestad: a pre-preliminary report, *Berichten van de Rijksdienst voor het Oudheidkundig Bodermonderzoek* 19: 183-207.

Van Es, W.A. (1990) Dorestad centred, in J. Bestemann, J. Bos and H. Heidinga (eds) *Medieval Archaeology in the Netherlands*, Assen, Van Gorcum: 151-82.

Van Es, W.A. and Verwers, W.J.H. (1980) *Excavations at Dorestad 1: The Harbour; Hoogstraat I*, Amersfoort, Nederlandse Oudheden 9.

Veyne, P. (1990) *Bread and Circuses: Historical Sociology and Political Pluralism*, Harmondsworth, Penguin.

Verhulst, A. (1977) An aspect of the question of continuity between antiquity and the Middle Ages: the origin of the Flemish cities between the North Sea and Scheldt, *Journal of Medieval History* 3: 175-206.

Verhulst, A. (1986a) La vie urbaine dans les anciens Pay-Bas avant l'an mil, *Le Moyen Age* XLI: 185-210.

Verhulst, A. (1986b) Les origines urbaines dans le nord-ouest de l'Europe: essai de synthèse, *Francia* 4: 57-81.

Verhulst, A. (1989) The origins of towns in the Low Countries and the Pirenne thesis, *Past and Present* 122: 3-35.

Verhulst, A. (1994) The origins and development of medieval towns in northern Europe, *Economic History Review* 47: 362-73.

Verhulst, A. and De Bock-Doehaerd, R. (1981) Nijverheid en handel, *Algemene Geschiedenis der Nederlanden* 1: 183-215.

Vince, A. (1990) *Saxon London: An Archaeological Investigation*, London, Seaby.

Wade, K. (1988) Ipswich, in R. Hodges and B. Hobley (eds) *The Rebirth of Towns in the West AD 700-1050*, London, Council for British Archaeology Research Report 68: 93-100.

Walmsley, A. (1995) Byzantine Palestine and Arabia: urban prosperity in Late Antiquity, in N. Christie and S. Loseby (eds) *Towns in Transition*, Aldershot, Scolar Press: 126-58.

Ward-Perkins, B. (1988) The towns of northern Italy: rebirth or renewal? In R. Hodges and B. Hobley (eds) *The Rebirth of Towns in the West AD 700-1050*, London, Council for British Archaeology: 16-27.

Ward-Perkins, B. (1996) Urban survival and urban transformation in the Eastern Mediterranean, in G.P. Brogiolo (ed.) *Early Medieval Towns in the Western Mediterranean; Ravello, 22-24 September 1994*, Mantua, Padus: 143-53.

Ward-Perkins, B. (1997) Continuitists, catastrophists, and the towns of Post-Roman Northern Italy, *Papers of the British School at Rome* 65: 157-76

Waywell, G.B. and Wilkes, J.J. (1995) Excavations at the ancient theatre of Sparta 1992-94, *Annals of the British School at Athens* 90: 436-60.

Weber, M. (1989) *The Protestant Ethic and the Spirit of Capitalism*, London, Fontana.

Whitelock, D. (1955) (ed.) *English Historical Documents, I, c. 500-1042*, London, Sidgwick & Jackson.

Whittaker, R. (1990) The consumer city revisited: the *vicus* and the city, *Journal of Roman Archaeology* 3: 110-18.

Wickham, C. (1984) The other transition: from the ancient world to feudalism, *Past and Present* 103: 3-37.

Bibliography

Wickham, C. (1994) Italy and the early Middle Ages, in C. Wickham, *Land and Power: Studies in Italian and European Social History, 400-1200*, London, British School at Rome: 99-118.

Wickham, C. (1997) The feudal revolution: comment IV, *Past and Present* 155: 196-207.

Wickham, C. (1998) Overview: production, distribution and demand, in R. Hodges and W. Bowden (eds) *The Sixth Century: Production, Distribution and Demand*, The Hague, E.J. Brill: 279-92.

Wood, I.N. (1986) Disputes in late fifth- and sixth-century Gaul, in W. Davies and P. Fouracre (eds) *The Settlement of Disputes in Early Medieval Europe*, Cambridge, Cambridge University Press: 7-11.

Wood, I. (1994) *The Merovingian Kingdoms* London, Longman.

Yorke, B. (1991) *Kings and Kingdoms of Early Anglo-Saxon England*, London, Seaby.

Index

Aachen, 35, 37, 65-6, 95; synods, 84
Abbasid caliphate, 35-6, 38, 58, 63, 96, 101, 123-4
Abu l'-Abbas, see Charlemagne's elephant
Adelhausen, 66
Aethelred (ealdorman), 113
African red slipware, 44
Aghlabid caliphate, 58, 63
Agobard of Lyons (bishop), 95
Albania, 40
Alcuin, 82
Aleppo, 101
Alfred (king), 84, 107, 112-13, 116-17, 124
Algarve, 44
Al-Mahdi (caliph), 36
Almere trade route, 106
Alpertus of Metz, 106
Alps, 36, 62, 64, 66, 123
Amorion, 47-8
amphorae, 42, 45, 47-8, 54, 57, 97, 105
Anastasius (emperor), 42
Anatolia, 47-8; fortress cities, 47, 60
Ancyra, 47
Anglo-Saxon England, 83, 107, 109, 112, 115-16
Anglo-Saxon kings, 95
'Anjar, 49-51, 80-1, 101
Antioch, 51
Apremont hoard, 62
Arabs, 36-8, 40, 44, 46, 118; Arab invasions, 17, 21-2, 43

Arhus, 76
Asia Minor, 89
Asser, 112
Augustine of Hippo (saint), 15-16, 70, 86
Augustus (emperor), 36, 121
Austrasians, 20
Avar treasure, 58

Baalbek (Lebanon), 49, 101
Baghdad, 51, 59
Balkans, 41-2, 48
Baltic sea, 38, 118, 124
Battle of Poitiers, 35
Beauvais, 97
Beirut, 49, 80
Belgium, 98
Belvezet hoard, 62
Benedict of Nursia (saint), 72, 86
Benedictines, 84, 96
Berytus (Beirut), 49
Birka, 74-5
Bismarckian nationalism, 20
Bloch, Marc, 16, 73, 75, 84-5
Boethius, 84
Bonn, 88
Brescia, 29, 60-1, 86, 123
British School at Rome, 28
Buecher, Karl, 18
Bull Wharf, 114
Burgred (king of Mercia), 117
Butrint, 40-3, 46, 61
Byllis, 42

142

Index